How to Get an Executive Job After 40

How to Get
an Executive Job
After 40

CHARLES S. MINER

COLLIER BOOKS · *New York, New York*

LIBRARY OF CONGRESS CATALOG CARD NUMBER: 63-16549

FIRST COLLIER BOOKS EDITION 1968
Second Printing 1971

This Collier Books edition is published by arrangement with Harper & Row, Publishers, Incorporated

The Macmillan Company
866 Third Avenue, New York, N.Y. 10022
Collier-Macmillan Canada Ltd., Toronto, Ontario

Printed in the United States of America

CONTENTS

How to Get an Executive Job After 40

1

YOU CAN GET A JOB

There is an executive job for you somewhere, but you will have to look for it, and the search may not be easy. You have handicaps, not the least of which is your maturity. Yet, properly exploited, that onetime liability can be transformed into a present-day asset.

Age discrimination has not been eliminated, but it has been breached. No longer is it a wall against which many a good man has pounded in frustration. Middle age is not a barrier to executive employment; it is an obstacle. And obstacles can be hurdled. You, however, must do the hurdling because you are the runner. Others may give you advice and cheer you on from the side lines, but it is you alone who will dash across the finish line.

There the analogy ends, because executive job search does not follow a cinder path or any other kind of track. There is no *one* right way to look for an executive position, but there are many time-tested pathways that lead there. Which one is best suited to you remains to be seen, and the quickest way to find out is to apply yourself to as many of them as possible.

Do not confuse desire for a new job with an ailment needing a cure—even if you are out of work. Unemployment is not a disease; it is a personal problem. So is being stuck in a job you do not particularly like, or one which has no future. The solution in each case lies in mapping out a campaign of action and then pressing forward on all fronts.

Do everything you can that will promote your job search. Get as many irons in the fire as possible, and when one cools have several more ready to take its place. You may get a job the first time you apply, but do not bank on it. Be prepared for a strenuous effort and you will be in for a pleasant surprise if you wind up in an attractive executive position after a brief campaign. But do brace yourself for a long haul, so you will not be *unpleasantly* surprised if the going turns out to be a little tougher than you expected.

The time to begin your executive job search, of course, is right now, and if you are permanently employed at the moment, so much the better. Everyone agrees that it usually is easier to get a new job when you have an old one, but this does not rule out the possibility of obtaining a position when you are unemployed. Men of your stature are doing it every day.

Like middle age, unemployment is no longer a barrier to a new executive job. It is merely another obstacle; one to be taken in stride. Appraise it for what it really is—a challenge to your ingenuity. You have met other problems head-on, and have overcome them. Now you are face to face with a new one. It is not fatal; it is not unchallengeable. It is just there, and you have to bowl it over before you can attain your job objective. That is all.

They say that "well begun is half done," and the place to begin well in your job hunt as an unemployed executive is with your departure from the company terminating your services. Leave on friendly terms. That is a must. For once in your life, put on an act—if you have to. Undoubtedly you are chagrined at the turn of events. You are less than human if you are not unhappy. Perhaps you feel, and maybe rightly so, that you have not had a square deal. You may even be convinced that you have been double-crossed. But true or not, keep those thoughts strictly to yourself.

Remember this: Your job has ceased, but your relationship to your erstwhile employer will continue to dog your footsteps so long as you are in the market for executive employment. Therefore, you must leave nothing undone to surround that relationship with a permanent aura of cordiality. Be cordial yourself, and act as if your former boss is too, even if he is not. Chances are he will be—he also is an executive, you know—but in any event be sure to conduct yourself, in his presence and out of it, as though he were one of your three or four best friends. As the politicians learn at the very start, it never pays to let a man know you think he is against you; least of all, an important man.

When the day of your departure finally arrives, say goodby in person to all of the top executives with whom you have had more than passing contact in the company for which you have been working. The logical procedure is to start with the highest man—the company president as a rule—and work your way down. Have something nice to say to each one. Thank those you worked for, getting across in a few words your gratitude for what you have learned under their tutelage. Be equally friendly with the others. Make a point of saying that your association with them has been both pleasant and instructive.

In each case, say what you have to say, and then get out as quickly as the limits of courtesy permit. It is courteous and definitely essential to sit down for a moment and indulge in a friendly chat if one of the bosses extends such an invitation. Do not hang around if he does not. Probably he will, however, and you owe him the return favor of standing up and making a graceful exit as soon as it becomes apparent that he has had his say.

Make friendly comments only. Do not explain your feelings or your attitude about aspects of your case which may have put you in something less than an elated mood. This is no time for post-mortems. Neither is it a proper occasion for requests. Do not ask for recommendations, or hint that you hope they will put in a good word for you whenever they have a chance, or express any misgivings about your future. Assume the air of one who regards himself as being in nothing more than a period of transition. Without saying so, act as though you expect anything in the way of a good reference or a job tip-off or any other kind of assistance to be extended automatically.

Above all, do not apologize for any fancied past failures on your part. Doubts may crop up even at this late date if a terminating boss can look at you and see anything less than a confident, capable executive embarking on a new venture. His confidence in you cannot possibly be any greater than your own, so make your final impression a good one—and a lasting one. It could be an important factor in determining how strongly the firm will go to bat for you when an opportunity arises.

As you close the door of the last job behind you, a completely new horizon comes into view. You must get ready to face many prospective employers, one of whom will hire you. And in one sense, at least, your unemployment can be a help. You can start on a new job immediately. Employed executives usually have to give two to four weeks' notice to their company.

You have noted the importance of not rehashing an old story in your farewells to the company you are leaving. Do not fight the battles over again in your mind, either. Let the past bury its dead. School yourself not to worry about things you cannot change: What has already happened is beyond alteration. Take heart from the knowledge that you do have plenty of company. Many a top-flight executive has had to start over again in middle age.

One thing you can do is resolve not to repeat any important mistakes that may have had a bearing on the loss of your last job. Make it a mental reservation, however, not an oral one. In substance, determine that you will make yourself so valuable to your new employer that he will be unable to do without your services no matter what happens. Then go to it, fortified by your awareness that executive unemployment is part of the process of business evolution in the United States.

It is a changing thing, in which one company gets bigger while another shrinks—or perhaps disappears entirely. One executive position evaporates while another one—or perhaps several—emerge into being. You have to change as the times change, and part of that process involves developing sufficient resiliency to switch from one job to another. It can be done. It is being done. You can do it.

You have every right to feel disappointed at facing a job hunt in your mature years. You need feel no disgrace. It happens every day, to men as good as you are. The four big job destroyers—mergers, changes of management, new money in the company, and realignment of staff—inflict no discredit on their victims.

Mergers almost always are arranged for the avowed purpose of trimming expenses, with payrolls high on the list. Executive positions rate at the very top, and it is virtually inevitable that some heads will roll. It is your misfortune that yours was one of them, but nothing more.

The House of Representatives Select Committee on Small Business reports that the 500 largest American industrial concerns took over 3,404 other companies in a ten-year period. Lots of executive jobs went down the drain in that process. Total business volume grew steadily, nevertheless, and there are even more executive jobs as a result.

When to Start

One of those jobs is for you, and as soon as you have stamped out any feeling of self-pity, eliminated fear, and analyzed away resentment, you are in the proper frame of mind to do it justice—once you have found it. You may wonder, though, when to start looking. Should you plunge into your job hunt immediately, or should you take a vacation first? There are many pros and cons to be evaluated, and you alone can make the final decision.

A vacation may be just the thing if you have not had one for a long time and can force yourself to enjoy it without letting your thoughts constantly revert to the problem of attaching yourself to a payroll in the kind of a position you want to fill. Assuming that you can do that, the vacation may be long or short, depending on your financial condition. You will come back mentally and physically refreshed in either case.

Do not take a between-jobs vacation if you have to admit to yourself that you are just stalling; that you dread the ordeal of a job search and are using this as an excuse to postpone it as long as possible. That attitude calls for self-administered mental therapy, and there is no better form of treatment than getting started on your job hunt the minute you walk out of your old office.

Besides, executive job-hunting is not nearly so formidable as it sounds. The pendulum is swinging in your direction now. Demand for experienced management is on the increase. Surveys show that four out of five American corporations habitually need at least one new executive. Many of these firms try to postpone hiring as long as they can, but the pressure of competition is forcing more and more of them to act quickly. The source of supply also is steadily shrinking—to your advantage—because younger executives are no longer so plentiful, proportionately, as they once were. Military service and the growing trend for more advanced education are steadily thinning out the supply of youthful brain power. The potential executive now gets started on his higher schooling about two years later than his father did, and he probably stays in college two to four years longer. He is the better for it, and so is the nation, but industry cannot wait indefinitely. It needs executive talent today. It needs men like you.

The opportunity is there, and you have powerful allies in your campaign to seize it. No less an authority than the American Medical Association has collected a wealth of evidence proving that the mature man can and will strive harder, stay on the job longer, and work more efficiently than most of his younger rivals.

A seven-year study by this authoritative medical organization confirmed that older men have far more to offer than the obvious assets of broader experience and keener judgment. They display greater loyalty, switch jobs less frequently, take less time off, achieve better safety records, are more devoted to their work, and get more done in the course of a day.

"Usefulness is not determined by age," says Professor John Neuner in his course on office management principles at the Bernard M. Baruch School of Business and Public Administration of the City College of the City University of New York. Supporting his declaration is a series of surveys undertaken by the National Association of Manufacturers and the University of Illinois, which disclosed that the frequently offered reasons for not hiring older men mostly lack foundation.

Among the myths exploded by the NAM are the outmoded beliefs that middle age increases absenteeism, aggravates safety hazards, lowers production, and decreases versatility. Quite the contrary. The mature executive definitely has much to his credit that in former days was accepted as exclusively the prerogative of the young. Characteristics widely taken as the "disabilities of age" are beginning to be recognized as the "abilities of maturity."

Experience Pays Off

The American Management Association also is the source of much valuable information for the job-hunting executive and is a stalwart booster of the growing movement to utilize the brain power of the man who has the priceless asset of experience.

More and more employers are heeding the AMA's emphasis on the importance of buying "quality" when they hire executive talent, and they recognize that proven experience is an essential ingredient of executive capacity. Charles Luckman, executive and architect who made Lever House one of the show-places of New York City, put it this way to columnist Bob Considine:

"Kids are great, but somebody's got to lend the substance of experience to their dreams." He added that he had recently taken on two new partners, and that in one case he specifically advertised: "Nobody under fifty-eight need apply." In this case the man he engaged as a partner was in fact fifty-eight years old.*

Then there is R. H. Richards, vice president of the International Shoe Company, who captured newspaper headlines from coast to coast when he told the Associated Press that "American industry stands to benefit when the old bugaboo of not hiring men over forty-five years of age goes down the drain where it belongs."

Mr. Richards, who was sixty-one years old at the time, declared, "It has been our experience that men in this older age bracket are reliable, do their work well, are easier to work with and, above all, have sounder judgment than many younger men."

Nor are such views any longer representative of isolated schools of thought. The Hastings College of Law in San Francisco gained nationwide attention by refusing to hire a teacher less than sixty-five years old. The average age of the school's seventeen faculty members was given as seventy-three, with forty-two years' experience teaching law.

"Barriers against older job seekers are breaking down," wrote the *Wall Street Journal* † after a study of nationwide employment trends. "An increasing number of employers are concluding that such restrictions—many of which date from the depression practice of giving preference in hiring to younger men with families—don't make much sense now."

Former President Dwight D. Eisenhower pointed up the importance of awakening to realities when he said: "Our nation now must learn to take advantage of the full potential of our older citizens—their skills, their

* *New York Journal American,* November 7, 1962.
† January 7, 1963.

wisdom and their experience. We need these traits fully as much as we need the energy and boldness of youth." *

Broad employment studies by Temple University, by the publishing company of Prentice-Hall, and by the National Office Management Association all confirm that corporations can and do save money by hiring mature executives, since they are prone to make a career of the post once they get it. Unlike younger men, they are not constantly looking around for a better position somewhere else.

Similar studies have proved time and again that the middle-aged executive is more likely to arrive at the office earlier, stay later, put in more hours at home working on his employer's problems, ask for less time off, and concentrate on doing his particular job better while sticking to it.

Whether you realize it or not, the fact is that when you get your job you probably will fill it better and hold it longer than a man ten years younger than you. Fortunately, you need not advertise the point because powerful groups are doing the advertising for you—and are aiming at the companies you will approach in your job search.

For instance, *Advertising Age,* forceful spokesman for Madison Avenue, is one of numerous management publications in every field continually stressing the importance of not letting the great reservoir of mature executive talent go to waste. They know how shortsighted it is to write off middle-aged management.

"Our economy can no longer afford this waste of talent and skill," wrote H. Clifton Morse and Lee McCafferty in *Personnel,* Sept.-Oct. 1962, an American Management Association publication. Pointing out

* *Employment of Mature Workers,* pamphlet published by National Association of Manufacturers, September 1960.

that our resources of executive manpower are "far from ample," the writers added, "Practical experience, good judgment, and a visible record of accomplishment are assets that far from being diminished by age are its natural consequences."

Much essential missionary work also is being done in your behalf as a mature executive by unimpeachable authorities who are disproving the mistaken idea that it costs more to fit an older man into a company pension plan, to cover him with insurance, and to supply the normal fringe benefits that go with modern-day executive employment.

Pension Plans No Problem

National associations, trade groups, chambers of commerce, universities, and foundations have checked the facts exhaustively, and they unite on one conclusion: There is no real monetary obstacle to including the mature employee in pension funds, group life insurance policies, hospitalization plans, medical protection, and similar components.

The AMA gave wide publicity to a U.S. Department of Labor report prepared in cooperation with a group of pension consultants, life insurance companies, bank trust officers, and educators, which revealed that the so-called pension "problem" for older people is really no problem at all. Here are four of the main points:

1. Most private pension plans provide retirement benefits based on years of service rather than a flat amount or a percentage of earnings unrelated to service.

2. Steady accrual of vested rights in private pension plans enables more older men to take new jobs without forfeiting pension credits already acquired.

3. Social security benefits make it unnecessary for

employers to provide substantial pensions in addition to what an older man earns during his necessarily abbreviated new employment.

4. The difference in cost between pensions paid to employees hired at an older age and those hired when younger will probably turn out to be much less than is anticipated. The younger man may prove to have a greater life expectancy after retirement, with resulting heavier costs to his employer.

This study opens up a point many employers formerly overlooked. The mature executive may prove even less costly in the long run. Many young employees "growing up" with the firm will live longer than actuarial tables now predict. Naturally, the longer they live the more benefits they draw from the pension fund.

In a similar vein, the National Association of Manufacturers analyzed a study by the Bureau of Labor Statistics and came up with this conclusion in its pamphlet *Employment of Mature Workers:* "Selective hiring of older workers will add only a small percentage of one per cent to management's total costs and may not add anything to the final cost of retirement benefits."

Another NAM pamphlet, *The Productive Years— Ages 45–65,* cites a study of pension plans in the steel industry which revealed that "for salaried workers, *the annual normal cost for young entrants is greater than for old entrants."*

The NAM also has some interesting citations from other studies. Among other things it refers to a Temple University survey on the employment of older people in Pennsylvania industries which showed that with respect to insurance costs, the net difference between premiums at age thirty and age fifty was negligible.

An actuary for the Equitable Life Assurance Society, questioned by the NAM about group insurance, said, "While costs generally move upward with age, the increases are relatively small when compared to salary costs."

After a review of all the facts, the NAM learned that "age is not considered by most insurance companies in determining health insurance premiums. While the duration of illness (or hospital stay) may be longer with mature people, they usually have fewer dependents and are less likely to require maternity benefits."

Finally, the NAM concluded: "The more one examines pension and insurance costs, the less valid they become as legitimate barriers to the employment of mature workers. When one considers the many personal assets the mature employee brings to the job, pension and insurance costs certainly lose whatever significance they may appear to have." *

These are but a few of the many arguments in your favor, but you need not—in fact you should not—advance them yourself. Never argue with the man whose payroll you are trying to join. Leave the debating to others, who are constantly selling these points where they will do the most good; with business leaders who hire men with talents such as yours.

So go out for that executive job. It is waiting for you. All you have to do is track it down. Good hunting!

* *The Productive Years—Ages 45–65,* pamphlet published by National Association of Manufacturers.

2

INVENTORY YOUR ASSETS

Now that you have decided to look for a new executive job, the time has come to size yourself up. Take stock of your talents, because you are selling yourself in a buyer's market and what you have to offer will be exhaustively scrutinized. Fortify yourself by reviewing your career from beginning to end.

This is also the ideal time to consider a change of direction if what you have been doing is not your favorite job. Since you are looking for a new position anyway, you have a great opportunity to press for the type of work you would most like to do. Perhaps the pressure of day-to-day responsibilities has forced your most cherished hopes into the background. If that is the case, here is the chance at last to aim at the job you really want. Balance salary with opportunity, but do not let ambition take the place of happiness.

First, however, you must relearn all there is to know about your business capabilities, and there is no better way than to go over your employment background. Start with the day you first earned money selling newspapers or running errands and make a written note of every job you ever held. The record will help you get an objective view of yourself.

Trace the steady development of your employment from the after-school paper route, or whatever it was, through the soda-jerking stint at the corner drugstore, and so on. Write down something about whatever you did that brought in money. Pinpoint it by location and, to the extent that memory permits, by dates. Note the steady progression in salary, adding a line or two to explain any hills and valleys.

You landed your first full-time job when? That is an important point; be sure to list it carefully, with a brief summary of what you did. Write down the name and address of the employer, the name and title of your boss, when you started, when you left (and why), your starting salary, and what you were being paid when you moved on. The exact details may escape you for the moment, but be as accurate as you can.

Then go on to the next job and do the same thing. Continue the record right up to your present post, or the last job you held. Do not leave any of your jobs out of this personal history. Each one contributed something to the process of molding you into today's executive.

A lot of this information may not interest a prospective employer, but you are making a *self-appraisal*, and everything you have done in the past has a bearing on the kind of executive you are now. Besides, concise data on each job you held after you were fully grown probably will have to be reported in the application form most employers require of every job seeker, right up to the highest executive. It will pay you to have the information clearly in mind so that you can whiz through the questionnaire with no delays or missteps.

When you have finished this, go over it again to probe for errors or omissions; if you find any, write them in immediately while they are fresh in your mind. By the time you are certain you have your complete employment record down in black and white you probably will have memorized the details, but carry a list in your pocket whenever you have an interview or make a job application. You want to be one hundred per cent accurate in everything you say or write, so take no chances.

Now your employment list is out of the way. You have a chronological record of your money-earning career from boyhood days to the present. You have refreshed your memory about your past experience, and recalling even the earlier part-time jobs will help you draw a complete picture of yourself.

Those very early school-day jobs, are they really important? They are to you, so do not let yourself forget them. Maybe you worked because family circumstances made it necessary. All right. You pitched in and did a job instead of having a good time. While other boys were playing ball, you were caddying at a golf club. You learned to shoulder responsibility early in life.

Or perhaps a job was not really necessary. You earned some spending money for yourself instead of looking to your parents for a bigger allowance. Self-reliance is a fine trait, and you developed it when you were still young.

Again, it may be that most of your school-day

friends had jobs, and you did not like to be the odd man in the crowd; so you got one too. Nothing wrong with that. In fact, it is admirable to go along with a constructive trend, and you are to be congratulated for recognizing that truth so quickly.

As you get closer to the present you will have more facts to recite in your personal business biography. Include everything about your recent employment that you consider out of the ordinary. Go over your career again and again to comb out precise duties which are *executive* as distinct from *clerical*. A once-over-lightly treatment will never do because you are bound to overlook something.

Emphasize the *responsibility* elements of the positions you have held. Others may have performed tasks assigned to them by you. Give yourself credit for being responsible for seeing that they were done properly.

Executives are decision-makers. List important decisions you made that had a bearing on your employer's success. Add ideas you originated, campaigns you inaugurated, and economies you effected. What you did yourself or had others do for the company's benefit is an integral part of your executive career. Include every one of them in your employment record.

Catalog Your Education

Your business career is not the only factor that molded you into an executive. Your education may have played an important role in shaping you into what you are today. Of course, if you worked your way up without the benefit of a college education you have done something exceptional and you should stress this at the appropriate time. Right now, you are recapitulating your assets, and lack of a college education is not in that category.

Most executives are university graduates, and if you belong in that majority write down a summary of your schooling, naming all the colleges, universities, and special schools you attended. List the degrees you earned, and state what you majored in at each school.

Did you graduate *magna cum laude*? Write it down. Are you a wearer of the Phi Beta Kappa key or a member of any other honor fraternity? Then mention it in your personal inventory. Did you take a postgraduate course without earning an advanced degree? Write down that you took so many years of postgraduate work in such and such a university, anyway. Did you take a correspondence course, or undertake special studies as a member of the armed services? They belong in your educational record.

Include any scholarships you won during your high school or college career. Add any special studies you undertook under a grant from a foundation or professional society. Write it down if you are a CPA or a member of the bar, along with every other phase or corollary of your educational background.

List Your Achievements

What you have so far is your employment record and your educational career, but you need more than that. The business world is full of men who worked and studied as long as you did, but never reached executive stature. You, however, are an executive, and that is a real achievement. So make past achievements the next order of business.

Get your writing paper handy, and cast your thoughts back to the earliest occasion when you were proud of yourself. It may seem trifling now, but it was important then. And do start as far back as possible.

The day you got your first bicycle may have been an outstanding moment of your early life, but getting it was no achievement if it was a birthday present; it was, if you bought it with money you earned yourself.

The test is, were you proud merely of the new bicycle or were you proud of the bike *and* of the fact that you got it because you earned it?

If it truly represented an achievement, write it down. Then write down other achievements which were important at the moment even if, seemingly, they lost some of their glamour as time went by.

There are all sorts of such achievements that justify notation. Passing your first-class test as a Boy Scout, becoming a patrol leader, or being elected captain of a basketball team are typical examples. Gaining the honor roll at high school, graduating as valedictorian, serving as class president, or editing the school paper are others.

Anything above the run-of-mine level in college rates attention, not forgetting extracurricular activities. If you headed a fraternity, you did well. You may have played the lead in a college play, or won a letter in football, or captured first prize in an oratorical contest.

Perhaps you did none of those things because you were the studious type who concentrated on getting high marks and extra credits that went to help you earn an advanced degree in a shorter time. Those good marks, those extra credits, that degree represent ambition and brains. You were tenacious. All of them belong on your achievement list.

For many a man, such achievements were out of reach simply because he did not have the chance. He had to work his way through college, and the job that produced tuition money left but scant time for study and none at all for other activities. Did you pay your own educational freight? Then you really achieved something. Write it down.

Inevitably, the day arrived when your school days ended and your business career began. Did you get your first job despite formidable competition from other applicants? That is achieving something, all right, so write it down.

Did promotions come rapidly? Were more responsibilities entrusted to you? Did you leave a well-paying job with limited horizon to accept a lower salary elsewhere in a post with greater future possibilities? Did another employer lure you away with a better position? Did you hike your company's profits? Reduce expenses? Develop new products? Simplify procedures? Land new contracts?

Or did you go into business for yourself, and make a success? Was your company bought over by a larger one in which you were given an executive position? Were you chosen for one or more important managerial posts? Were you elected a member of the board of directors? Did you speak for the company at important gatherings?

You are getting into the realm of bread-and-butter achievements now; the kind your future new employer is willing to pay money to have duplicated. Such executive attributes bring cash into the company's till. Some of your achievements in nonbusiness fields also can bring the company prestige—and often money, too—because a firm looks well when its executives are highly rated in their communities and in professional circles. In that connection, do not forget that service in the armed forces has added luster to many a businessman's lifetime career.

Some of the personal achievements worth noting are membership in prestige clubs, official positions in important community organizations, appointive or elective offices in local governmental bodies, and citations awarded by service organizations or professional associations.

You will have a pretty substantial list of achievements by the time you have brought your history up to date. With it, and with your educational and employment record, you have a pattern by which you next proceed to cut the cloth that will fit the job you seek.

Study all the material intently. As you pore over it you will see an executive emerge; a man who is more capable in some things than in others; who can do this better than he can do that; and who was happier when he was active in such and such a position than when he served in any other capacity.

You have found yourself now, so stop reading and start writing again. Write down what you consider the ideal position for you to fill. Outline the duties and the responsibilities you would *like* to assume, leaving out nothing you think is important but wasting no time and space on extraneous matters.

And stick to your job. Of course you would like to be president of General Motors or the Standard Oil Company. You would also like to be President of the United States, for that matter, but you are looking for a job suited to your talents and, at the same time, to your inclinations.

Imagine that you have been offered employment where you have been told you can write your own ticket insofar as the particular position you will fill is concerned. Take into account your good points and your shortcomings, and with all the facts now at your fingertips blend your qualifications into a blueprint of the position that would give you scope for your greatest capabilities—and would bring you the most satisfaction.

Put down everything tangible that comes to mind about the duties and responsibilities of your job. You will be thwarting your own efforts if you digress to comment on other features, such as an agreeable chief, or cooperative associates, or hard-working subordinates. Stick to your goal, which is the job you want and are determined to get.

Your first draft is apt to be lengthy and disjointed. Rewrite it, eliminating something here, perhaps adding something there, rearranging this and that, and generally improving the language. Keep on rewriting the job description—and condensing it. Before long you will have it down to one paragraph containing a wealth of information. When it has been completed to your satisfaction you probably will have something about as long as the Lord's Prayer. Let us hope that, insofar as your job hunt is concerned, it is half as comprehensive.

This short description of the ideal job you have conjured up was written for your own eyes, just as was the material on which it is based. Compare it with your experience, your education, and your achievements. If all four dovetail neatly—and they probably will—you are ready to proceed. Otherwise, you will have to amend the job description, because the other three elements are beyond change. Revise the job description, if necessary, until it portrays the type of executive your background has created.

Once this has been achieved, you have in your hands a description of your job objective and documentary material substantiating your right to claim such a job. This you must now condense into a résumé for presentation to prospective employers.

3

DRAW YOUR PERSONAL IMAGE

Your résumé may take any one of a variety of forms, but it must convince the employer you are the man to fill the job you seek. It must also be written so that he will read it, which means that you must write enough about yourself—but not too much. You must be specific while being careful not to strap yourself into a strait jacket. You must be comprehensive without getting lost in generalities, and you must be factual without being dull.

This is a tough assignment you have given yourself. You are drawing up your executive specifications, and you must do so in a way that will induce the market for your services to inspect the product.

Types of Résumés

Executive employment experts have narrowed the résumé field down to four basic styles which experience has proven are the most effective. They are the functional, the chronological, the company, and the narrative.

The *functional* résumé (see pp. 41–43) stresses the important job elements a prospective employer will want to know about before he is willing to call you in for an interview. In it you emphasize your major experience and your notable successes in specific executive positions you have held. This type of presentation is favored by more authorities than any other.

In the *chronological* résumé (see pp. 44–47)you list every job you have held throughout your business career, beginning with the most recent one and working back. The name of each employer must be given and so must the title of each job you held. Naturally, you give more space to the more important posts, and you emphasize your valuable contributions to the employer.

Mature executives can be pardoned for disliking this style, since the necessary dates automatically expose the writer's age. Consequently, it is not often submitted except upon request. However, such a request usually is made if a less revealing résumé has attracted the interest of an employer or employment agency. Therefore, you should write one and have copies always available.

If you have a liking for this particular presentation you may write one with the years omitted, but this can be dangerous if you have worked for numerous employers over the years. You may unwittingly stamp yourself as either an old "fuddy-duddy" or a floater who drifted from one job to another.

The *company* résumé is similar to the chronological approach except that the various concerns you have worked for are not necessarily listed in strict time sequence. You name all the employers but only your highest job title in each firm and, of course, you start with the most important position regardless of when it was held.

Literary talent is necessary to produce an effective *narrative* résumé, which is a feature article about yourself. It is the modern successor to the letter of application that was used before résumés became standard, and in the hands of a good narrator it is hard to beat. It must be concise, and it is so hard to turn out a real masterpiece that it should be shunned by all save the gifted writer.

Except for the narrative type, whatever résumé style you adopt requires a *pro forma* introduction. Some experts recommend a "thumbnail sketch," which should epitomize your talents in such a way as to draw a picture of your job objective while simultaneously describing you as the very man to fill the post—preferably in not more than thirty-five or forty words.

One school of thought holds that a mere condensed description of the job objective is sufficient, *provided* the accompanying text amply supports the thesis that you can do what you say you want to do. Your résumé will not be worth the paper it is written on unless it does do just that, but there is no harm in summarizing your personal qualifications at the same time.

In any case, you should write the introduction *last*. Get the body of your résumé completed to your satisfaction—which is bound to take time—and then develop your thumbnail sketch or your job objective into an effective lead for the supporting material. If you decide on a straight, job objective description, it will have to be shorter than the one you wrote after you completed your job history and your achievement list. The suggested ceiling of forty words has lots of merit.

However, having temporarily sidetracked the introduction, you begin with the résumé itself, and you immediately find you have a lot more leeway if you do a functional job, because you can start right off with the most important thing you have to say—just as a newspaper reporter does.

War has been declared, or a transcontinental plane has crashed, or three people died in an automobile accident. That is the kind of information the reporter puts in the first paragraph of his news story, and you cannot do better than follow his example. What if you did rise from office boy to general manager in one company? That is fine, but what will impress the prospective employer most are the *outstanding* achievements you racked up as general manager. Start telling him about them in the first sentence.

A good way to get off on the right foot is to imagine that you are an employer looking for an executive to fill the kind of job you want. Then list the principal requirements which will have to be met in their entirety by the successful applicant. Probably there will be five or six major points such an employer will stress, and these should be written down on the left-hand half of a sheet of paper. Opposite them, on the right-hand side, list your own accomplishments in each category. Add to this your proven capacity to handle the problems likely to arise in that connection. The sum total is the kind of information that belongs in your résumé.

As you translate your background data into a workable résumé, be sure to bear in mind that although your experience is behind you—where else could it be?—you still have an executive career ahead. Therefore, write as much as possible with the future in mind, lest your résumé read like a business obituary.

Do not waste space extoling routine things you have done, no matter how well you may have done them. Go easy on adjectives, too. No doubt some of your achievements were remarkable, but let the employer deduce that himself. You supply the evidence; he draws the conclusions; and they will be favorable where favor is merited.

In other words, your résumé must speak for itself; and it must speak on the management level because it is describing the abilities of a thoroughly experienced, highly trained executive. Because you are not a clerk or a trainee, it will be assumed that you are sober, hard-working, and industrious. You may plant the germ of doubt in the employer's mind if you go to the trouble of telling him you are.

Cite Specific Examples

It cannot be emphasized too strongly that the employer wants *specific* information about actual accomplishments; so you must list several that will add to your executive stature and kindle in him a desire to put your talents to work for him. Tell the man what you can do for him, and prove it by concrete examples of what you have done for others. Limit the examples to the most important ones. You can mention others in your interview, but so long as you are trying to persuade employers to see you, stress quality—not quantity.

Respect the employer's intelligence by being brief but spare his imagination by supplying enough information for him to evaluate you properly. If he is left to guess, he may guess wrong. Worse than that, he may decline to conjecture at all and turn his attention to another applicant.

Present your qualifications in the most favorable

light possible, but remember that true executives are never braggarts. Guard against inadvertently boasting that you have performed remarkable management feats; content yourself with making it plain that you *did* perform them.

Disregard space limitations for the present. Condensation, consolidation, and elimination will come later. Right now you are putting into résumé form what heretofore has been a conglomeration of notes.

When you have exhausted the source material you compiled about your *job objective,* report on your other experience—again with emphasis on the more important points. Hit only the highlights of work you did that need not necessarily have had a direct bearing on your prospective new job but did play a part in molding you into an executive. You may be laying the foundation for a good "second choice" job, but do not say so. Let the employer note for himself that you are versatile. It is the mark of a seasoned executive.

Make this first draft a comprehensive document. Include full details about all important phases of your business background. Designate the products involved. Define the executive responsibilities you shouldered. Identify the industry, by all means. Make unmistakably clear the exact relationship of each of your jobs to the company's setup as a whole. You were part of a team; do not leave the prospective employer wondering if you were a tackle or a halfback.

Include any *special* skills you have. They may or may not have a direct bearing on the job you want, but they are certain to convey some impression of the type of executive you are. Limit yourself to pertinent skills, of course. You may shoot the best game of golf in six counties but do your talking about that at the nineteenth hole—not in your job résumé. It must cover only those special personal aptitudes that go to help a company get ahead in business.

The highlights of your educational background should be included, and so should any *noteworthy* achievements outside the realm of business, with two particular exceptions. Never mention your church affiliation or your fraternal connections, no matter how high you may have risen in these organizations.

Your domestic situation has to be covered, and it properly belongs near the end of the résumé. Employers usually want to know your basic family setup; so you have to tell them, but do not expand on the subject. Say you are married and have two children, or whatever the fact is, but do not add that you are supporting your mother. If you are a bachelor or a childless grass widower, write "single, no children." A childless widower may prefer to say "widower" instead of "single," and either is satisfactory, but there is no place in a job résumé for any hint of a divorce. Do not hide it; just keep it to yourself until the employer brings it up—if he ever does.

A divorced man with children should dismiss his status with a concise "have three children," or whatever the number is. Do not say anything about "adult" children. That flaunts your age, which is another thing you do not talk about until asked.

Then there is the matter of your health. If it is good, say so in two or three words. "Excellent health" fills the bill nicely. Add your elementary physical specifications such as height and weight if they support your claim to good health. Leave them out, if you have a paunch that will be prematurely disclosed by a figure that automatically denotes overweight. Omit the entire subject of health if you have an affliction of any kind that may act to your detriment even though your physician feels it is no threat to longevity so long as you live temperately.

At the very bottom write that you are willing to

relocate or travel—if you are. Say nothing on the subject if you are not.

With this final sentence you have concluded a detailed, factual, and possibly a ponderous document which contains the information the employer wants and, probably, considerable data he would willingly do without. Therefore, you must next proceed to separate the grain from the chaff; to make certain that you have put first things first; and to satisfy yourself that if you were an employer, you would hire the man described.

As an employer you would be less than enthusiastic about interviewing an applicant who assailed you with a sales presentation that failed to describe his experience smoothly, continuously, and logically. You might be perplexed, and possibly annoyed, at running across a statement that seemed out of place. You could be jarred completely out of an interviewing frame of mind if you found a paragraph which had no genuine bearing on the subject as a whole.

Make a note of such deficiencies as soon as your eye catches them. Remember, too, that the man described in the résumé is supposed to become increasingly clear the more you read. If his image gets blurred from time to time, the presentation has definitely missed the target. It will score a hit only if such a clear, single image has been presented that the employer is at once impelled to meet him.

You can look forward to interviews if such a picture has been drawn, but you have handicapped yourself seriously if it has not. Your chances are slight if your résumé arouses only a *vague* interest instead of making a distinct impression.

Hints on Résumé Designing

Your material is good, of course. What you have to

do now is package it more effectively Here are some time-proven résumé-designing tips:

Short statements, properly written, pack a stronger wallop than long ones, even though the latter may be equally well done. Shy away from phraseology that might belong in a college thesis but has no place in straight-from-the-shoulder management talk.

Each statement *must* punch home the point you are making. If it does not, write it over and over again until it registers emphatically. Of course, if there is no real point involved in a particular statement the proper remedy is to strike it out completely.

Résumé specialists continually tell their clients to be informative, factual, emphatic, and brief. Brevity beats verbiage every time. Keep the number of sentences down and use fewer words in each sentence— but be sure to say what is on your mind. You cannot afford to leave out important words, thereby dimming the message you are trying to convey; but you can frequently make one word express your meaning as well as two or three. Sometimes one word will turn the trick even better. For instance, "directed" is more effective than "was director of."

Guard against the tendency to overdo condensation by tucking two or three different subjects into a single paragraph. You may even find yourself trying to cover too much territory in one sentence. Protect yourself by dealing with one thing at a time. Divergent managerial responsibilities you shouldered, savings you effected, and records you accomplished must be separated, so that the employer can digest each one thoroughly without the distraction that comes from trying to figure out what boosting sales by $140,000 in six months has to do with trimming the budget by $150,000 in three years.

Start a new paragraph on the slightest provocation. Each statement that deals with something else that is beside the point covered just ahead of it deserves to stand alone. So does each sentence deserve to start with a bang. Begin, whenever possible, with an action verb, so that the important feature of the sentence will immediately capture the reader's attention. Do not rob yourself of a hit by rambling on with a remark that "after personal study of the company's personnel problem succeeded in reducing the payroll by $27,-000." Drive the point home at the outset by declaring you "reduced payroll by $27,000 after a personal survey."

Of course you must always be clear, because it is well known that anything that can be misunderstood probably will be misunderstood. Select your words carefully. Be satisfied only with those which are most informative yet most precise. But, again, do not let excessive zeal lead you onto dangerous ground. Technically precise terms belong only in résumés dealing with technical jobs. You do not use them when you are talking business with an executive. Talk business in your résumé, too, using the same kind of words the employer probably will use when he speaks to you.

Finally, spare no effort to make the résumé something to be proud of. Rearrange the paragraphs until the continuity strikes you as being the best that could be attained. Chop out everything that does not add force to your story. Be alert to insert any important point that may have inadvertently been overlooked. And do not hesitate to make changes A little extra time now may save you lots of disappointments later. Often, you can pep up your story tremendously just by finding better substitutes for a few key words.

Words to Avoid

Here are some words experienced job counselors warn *against*:

Extensive—Too vague; implies incomplete coverage. Give the exact scope of whatever you are describing.

Considerable—A weak term that means more than a little, but not very much. Say how much.

Administrative—Too weak for an executive's résumé. Handling the stamp box is administrative, and even an office boy can do that.

Inaugurated—Means merely that something somehow got started under you. Make it plain that you did the starting, or supervised it.

Competent—A weak adjective that sounds as if even you do not think you are any "great shakes" as an executive.

Qualified—Weak again. Suggests that you may be able to do something if given the chance. Do not be "iffy" about your talents.

There are countless more, but these illustrate the point. Re-examine each descriptive word in the draft, and substitute something better for every single one that is the least bit doubtful.

Then train your spotlight on the paragraph arrangement. The first one should cover the most important thing about you. That is a must. Write it so well that the employer will instantly learn your outstanding characteristic.

The second paragraph must drive home your second strongest personal asset. Apply the same thinking to succeeding paragraphs, so that each one makes a genuine impact—but in descending importance. And which are the most important? The ones that demonstrate how you will be most valuable to the employer, of course.

When your blue-penciling operation is finished, you have the foundation for an effective résumé. Your executive experience is summarized. Your outstanding qualifications are set forth in proper order and are proven by specific examples. The whole thing is composed of a series of coherent, closely related statements which, however, are neatly separated into paragraphs, so that there is plenty of white space on the sheet.

Now rewrite this document into a next-to-final draft, and as you copy it off, line by line, you probably will add a touch here and clip off something there because you will never run out of ideas. When it is finished, give it the final going over that will produce the sales pitch on which you will stand or fall in the employer's estimation when he compares it with the others he is studying before he decides just whom to interview for the position he has to offer.

Final Check List

A final check list drawn up by executive placement experts contains the following rules for your guidance in determining whether, at long last, you have created the résumé you need:

1. Is any paragraph too long? Have you violated the rule of "one at a time"? If so, break it up into subparagraphs.

2. Are all paragraphs in proper cumulative, informative sequence? Or should what you say later be brought up into a former topic in order to provide balance and increase effectiveness?

3. Is each sentence a dynamic jewel in itself? Or is one or more too long? Or do any of them open weakly instead of strongly? Have you weeded out every word that is meaningless or antagonistic? Have you eliminated redundancy? Is that one *best* word used where it should be?

4. Can the composition be made more effective by the use of captions and subcaptions? Or by eliminating them? Or by more imaginative use of indented paragraphing to bring related ideas together?

5. Does each paragraph logically lead to the next, even though somewhat unrelated ideas, biographical details, or job functions are covered? Would a complete rearrangement be more effective?

6. Is each individual item accorded proper emphasis and treated at its appropriate proportional length? Is a truly

important bit of information brushed off too quickly? Or is a matter of lesser importance given too much attention?

You must be convinced that each of these rules has been fully complied with before you can consider the résumé completed. When you are satisfied that you have done the best you can with it, study it again in conjunction with your previously written introduction. This must be rewritten to make it as short as practicable and to make sure it matches the body of the résumé, whether it is a thumbnail sketch or a job objective.

Whatever type you write, remember that the introduction must mirror the experience you have outlined and that the experience in turn must substantiate each assertion or objective expressed in the introduction.

Remember, too, that this short review goes at the very head of your résumé. It must tell the employer immediately that you are a controller, or an advertising manager, or an economist. He will be justifiably annoyed if he has to do a lot of reading to find out what work you do.

That brings up the all-important question of job titles. You must be specific about this because generalities in a headline never got anyone an executive job anywhere. Incidentally, the word "executive" is a handy thing to use in a passport where you have to state your profession and would like to get by with a single word, but it has little value in a job résumé. You have to be more concrete.

Here is a high-sounding opener, often cited as an example of what *not* to write:

Versatile executive with outstanding background; expert in increasing sales and developing products.

This is a picture of a man who claims he is good and perhaps he is—but in what way? What was his capacity? Sales manager? Marketing director? And that "outstanding background" of his: Was it in consumer goods? Heavy industry? Groceries? Pharmaceuticals? Or what?

Were those increasing sales of his achieved on retail or on wholesale levels? Were they regional or nation-wide? And how about naming a product or two that he developed. Or at least identifying the industry? In short, exactly what job does the man want, anyway?

The following sample illustrates the proper approach:

General sales manager—packaged consumer goods— national distribution.

This names the job title, the type of product, and its sales scope. That is covering a lot of territory in just eight words. Here is another:

Chief accountant—heavy in cost accounting and budget control—in multiplant manufacturing company.

More words there, but accounting is a comprehensive term, and a chief accountant has to pinpoint his back-ground at the outset. This man is versatile in his field, and he makes it plain without the use of adjectives. The employer knows precisely what the applicant is offering.

Your introduction, be it a thumbnail sketch or a job objective, must be equally plain. Of course, the above samples are merely the first line or two of condensed autobiographies. More is needed, but not much more. The general sales manager buttressed his heading with concise supporting information:

Skilled in training salesmen. Effectively managed trade promotions, opened new markets, established channels of distribution. Practical advertising experience.

You then know what he has done and what job he is

after. The ensuing text of the résumé proves his contentions and justifies his ambitions.

Note that the usual rules of grammar apply but little to résumés. In the introduction particularly, you use a staccato approach. These are your headlines. They tell what the story is about—just as "Paris-Bound Stratoliner 48 Hours Overdue" tells the newspaper reader that what follows is an account of a missing airplane. He will have to look for another story if he wants to know who won the election, or what the stock market is doing.

In brief, select your job title carefully—and be certain that you *do* name it in no uncertain terms. Then describe yourself and your experience in two or three dozen words. That is your introduction. What comes next is the body of your résumé. It should all be condensed into not more than two standard size typewritten pages, so do some more trimming if it runs over.

Typing the Résumé

Your résumé will have to be typed. There must be no misspelled words and no flagrant violations of the rules of elementary grammar, though the latter may be somewhat abridged. It must also be properly centered on the two pages—preferably with about the same number of lines on each. (See examples on pp. 41–43, 44–47.)

For the best-looking job, start about one inch from the top and type in your name, address, and telephone numbers—business and residential. You may center the name and address, as on a letterhead, in which case your business phone number should appear on one side of the sheet and your residence phone on the other.

Or you may put your name and address on the left-hand side of the sheet and the two telephone numbers on the opposite side. The choice is yours; just make certain that there is a neat balance.

Drop down about three-quarters of an inch and begin your thumbnail sketch or job objective. Use single space typing throughout, and leave margins of about one and one-quarter inch on each side for the body of the résumé. The introduction, however, should be indented an additional half-inch on each side so that it will be narrower and thus will stand out.

The thumbnail sketch is always headed by your job title in capital letters, underlined and centered. For example:

BRANCH MANAGER—

PACKAGED CONSUMER GOODS

However, if you are set on confining the introduction to a straight out-and-out job objective, center the words *Job Objective* so that they form the heading.

Next drop down another three-quarters of an inch and center the word *Experience*. Use your own judgment about writing it in capitals, but be sure it is underlined. Two lines below the word *Experience,* start your résumé text. All of the instructions so far are applicable to the functional, the chronological, and the company type of résumé.

Now let us take up the *text* of the functional résumé (pp. 41–43). You may indent the first line of each paragraph if you prefer, but the more common practice is *not* to indent except when you want to make a subparagraph stand out. In that case, indent *each* line of that particular subparagraph one-half inch. Here and there, underline an especially important word or phrase.

Double-space between each paragraph and each subparagraph so that there is ample white space around all of the individual groupings. Stop one inch from the bottom of the first page and continue on the second. Use the same type of spacing and margins on both pages.

If your experience covers various fields, insert short captions at appropriate places. Such captions as *Overseas Background* and *Liaison Experience* are useful. Less important background data can be grouped under the heading *Other Experience.*

Below your experience—allowing three spaces— you should list your major employers unless you already have identified them *by name* in the text itself. Many résumés refer to employers only by industry under the *Experience* heading and in that case you center the word *Affiliations* and then list them, starting two spaces lower. Where it is desirable to name more than two or three, they should be typed in two parallel columns, with a wide margin on each side so that they will catch the eye without running too deeply on the page.

Three spaces below that list comes *Education,* centered, unless you have only one school to report, in which case you use *Personal* and include your college, degree, etc. Where your educational background justifies separation, by all means give it a separate heading.

Functional Résumé

JAMES L. BLANK

Residence   1760 National Street   Office

MOrton 1-2345   Cleveland 81, Ohio   NEwton 5-6789

PRODUCTION MANAGER

Metal fabrication executive with profit-minded approach to progressive methods of organization, cost control, and expediting. Heavy in project management and contract negotiation. Industry's legislation representative.

EXPERIENCE

Management

Directed all activities of aluminum fabrication company engaged in supplying construction materials to multimillion-dollar industrial, institutional, and public works projects.

> Increased company's gross billings from $500,000 to more than $10,000,000 yearly, and its net worth from $50,000 to $425,000.

> Planned expediting methods and procurement policies and procedures for both manufacturing and purchasing.

> Determined personnel policies, directed training programs, and supervised organization planning. Revised pension, profit-sharing, and incentive payment plans.

Developed a unit cost control system of cost analysis designed to provide current labor costs quickly for prompt action at selected stages.

Production Control

Achieved record output in fulfillment of consumer-tailored prime contracts with top industrial and institutional clients.

> Cooperated effectively with client management to produce outstanding results for Western Electric, Ohio Oil, Allied Chemical, General Electric, Montgomery Ward, Remington Rand, and Litton Industries.

JAMES L. BLANK

Special Activities

Chairman for five terms of Public Relations Committee of the Ohio State Association of Manufacturers. Maintained legislative contacts to promote local business development and favorable taxes.

Served on special Tax Committee of Cleveland Board of Trade.

OTHER EXPERIENCE

General Management

Assistant vice president, reporting directly to the president of large construction company. Solved problems relating to improved purchasing procedures, production controls, distribution methods, departmental organization, and general administration.

Obtained refund of more than $2,000,000 in excess taxes and successfully defended against recapture by the government.

Reduced transportation costs by utilizing "piggyback" services, consolidated truck loads, stop-offs, and other devices for lowest cost per ton.

Negotiated many short-term government contracts to fill unused production time and preclude idle-time payments under "guaranteed workweek."

Reorganized purchasing department and buying methods to obtain greater efficiency by using specialists instead of general buyers.

AFFILIATIONS

General Aluminum Corp.   United Construction Co.

EDUCATION

Purdue University—M.E. Degree
Ohio State University—Took special courses in
business administration

PERSONAL

Born and raised in Keokuk, Iowa. Married, three children.
Member: Associated Architects & Engineers
Consulting Management Engineers
Ohio Contractors Association
Will travel or relocate in the United States.

Under *Personal,* set forth your family status, health (unless it is inadvisable to mention it), the various important offices you have held, the business or professional associations to which you belong, your important clubs, and your willingness—if you are willing —to travel and relocate.

That is the end.

Chronological and company résumés (see pp. 44–47) follow similar broad lines except that each job has to be listed—along with the name of the employer. Name the company and give the title of *each* of your jobs (with their duration by dates) in a chronological résumé. Give the firm's name and the title of your *highest* job in a company résumé. In all cases, either capitalize or underline company names and job titles so that they will stand out clearly. Location of the company usually is unnecessary, unless it is an overseas branch or subsidiary and you are aiming for a similar locale.

You will have an informative, neat-looking, impressive résumé when you reach the last line, but if you want to dress it up still more you can have your photograph photostated at the top at a cost of only a few dollars for the copies. Gummed photostamps are even cheaper and are handy to have around because you can paste them on special résumés you write from time to time.

Many executives use a photograph in one form or another for a variety of reasons. Pictures convey character, and they attract attention.

In any event, with or without a photo, a résumé is an effective key to unlock employment doors—if you use it wisely. Put yours to work for you.

Chronological Résumé

JOHN R. DOE
1776 Constitution Avenue   Telephones $\begin{cases} \text{Off.—LI 9-8765} \\ \\ \text{Res.—KE 4-2367} \end{cases}$
Boston 14, Massachusetts

Job Objective

Financial position as Controller or Treasurer of multiplant manufacturing and distribution organization. Emphasis on cost reduction and work simplification. Formulate special projects in purchasing, production control, marketing, and new product developments.

Experience

UNITED FOOD PRODUCTS, INC.   1948-1963

Controller of this national multiplant food manufacturing and distributing concern with annual sales of $150,000,000.

> Established and administered all accounting and internal audit policies and procedures; trained current headquarters staff and regional incumbents to free self for special management assignments.

> Organized newly acquired offices; prescribed standardized reporting procedures; installed centralized accounting system at head office.

> Member of executive profit-planning and product-pricing team established to maintain and assure satisfactory return on investment.

Earlier, as Assistant Controller, initiated and directed work-simplification programs to protect competitive position.

> Analyzed and interpreted periodic operating statements for executive and field management.

> Prepared SEC statements and annual reports to stockholders.

JOHN R. DOE
GENERAL BISCUIT COMPANY   1940-1948

Treasurer for four years of this old, well-established firm serving the grocery trade in New England. Was offered position of Executive Vice President when resigned to join United Foods.

> Prepared operating and capital expenditures budgets; coordinated manufacturing and sales

budgets; developed and maintained effective management controls.

Increased profit recovery through development of new uses for bakery waste materials and emptied containers.

When Controller, forecasted monthly profit and loss and then reviewed results and planned expanded or corrective measures.

NEW ENGLAND THRIFT MARTS, INC.   1938-1940

Chief Accountant of this local chain of self-service groceries. Introduced latest bookkeeping machines at a saving of more than $50,000 in two years.

Simplified cost accounting system. Eliminated wasteful reporting systems of individual stores. Centralized all tax accounting records in head office thereby reducing personnel.

Revised payroll accounting to effect economies and simplify office procedure.

MODERN BAKERS, INC.   1936-1938

Head Bookkeeper in this wholesale bakery. Reported direct to company President on purchasing, billing, and collections. Improved credit analysis at substantial saving to firm through weeding out doubtful accounts.

Declined offer of appointment as Treasurer when left to join the much larger New England Thrift Marts.

Education

Wharton School of Commerce—M.B.A. degree, 1936.

Dartmouth College—B.A. degree, 1932.

Personal

Born June 17, 1910, in Manchester, New Hampshire. Attended local public schools and Phillips Exeter Academy.

Worked way through Dartmouth by waiting on tables in restaurant and working as Director of Athletics in boys' camp in summer. Financed Wharton studies by coaching undergraduates at University of Pennsylvania.

Certified Public Accountant in New Hampshire and Massachusetts.

Past President of the Boston Chapter, Controller's Institute.

Member of Economic Club of Boston, Boston Chamber of Commerce, Boston Board of Trade, and Financial Executives Club.

Excellent health. 5' 10" tall, weigh 175 pounds.

Married, two children.

Will travel, relocate in U.S.A. or abroad.

4

WHEN AND WHERE TO START

Your completed résumé—the very best summary of your executive capabilities you have been able to prepare—is now in your hands. It is your sales pitch. It will get interviews for you, and it will help you perform better during such interviews. It will also speak for you when you are not around to do your own talking. But it will do none of those things unless you use it wisely. It is a marketing tool, but only a tool. You must do the wielding.

You have made up your mind what type of job you want. You also know that you will have to find it; the job will not come looking for you. And to find it you must canvass the territory where such jobs exist.

Africa is a great place for hunting, but you will never find a polar bear there. Executive jobs are similar captives of environment. You will find yours only where the men are doing the kind of work you do.

Lining up such job opportunities takes time, and the sooner you start, the better for you. And the time to start, obviously, is while you still have a job—if at all possible. Every authority agrees that it is easier to get a new job when you are working than when you are unemployed.

No matter how highly qualified an executive may be, he is making a mistake if he deliberately waits until he is out of work before he begins to make the rounds of prospective employers. He has not ruined his chances by any means, but neither has he helped them. Every worthwhile job opening is certain to attract numerous applicants; and, all other things being equal, the man who is still being paid for his talents usually gets prior consideration.

Few executives are surprised when they lose their jobs. Mergers are not consummated overnight. Bankruptcies do not come like a bolt from the blue. Business slumps take time to produce a devastating effect, and the executive worth his salt is quick to recognize it when his employer's financial condition approaches the stage where top-level personnel-pruning is in prospect.

The signs will be visible to everyone capable of reading the language of commerce, and the first hint should have the middle-aged executive throwing out job feelers before he even starts home for dinner that night. Often, you will not have to trust your own judgment. Your employer may give you advance notice—many do—that a new deal is in the offing in which your services, regrettably, will have no place. You may be told it would be well to start looking around for a new connection. "Something better" is the phrase usually employed.

Being on the management level, you are aware, of course, that your personal job search must not be allowed to interfere with your regular office duties. Your messenger boy may be pardoned for trying to improve his own fortunes on the company's time, but not you. The company comes first during office hours; your personal interests predominate the rest of the time.

The boss may be kind enough to tell you there is no objection on his part if you devote a reasonable amount of office time lining up a new job. Be thoughtful enough, in return, to decline with thanks except for rare occasions when an important interview is set for a morning or an afternoon. When that happens, tell your chief—not your secretary or his—that you would like to leave the office long enough to keep the appointment, and offer to make up the time.

The prospective employer who is interviewing you will assume that you have made the necessary arrangements in your own office; so you need not tender him any explanations. Canvassing for a new job when you ought to be hard at work in your present position is a totally different matter. That looks too much as if you were cheating on your present employer, and the man you are talking to may wonder if you might not do the same thing after you get on his payroll. What he wants is an executive with a reputation for devoting *all* his working hours to the company paying his salary.

Consequently, you must carry out your job search at night and on week ends, and keep your daytime legwork down to the minimum. By carefully budgeting your time you will be surprised at how much territory you can cover and still do more than you are being paid for in your own company.

Get Personal Recommendations

The next question that arises is *where* to start, and the answer is that your initial efforts should be directed to *important* men who know you well and are aware of your ability. Such men may not have job openings; they may not even be in a line of business where you could fit in at all, but the personal recommendation of a business leader big enough to swing a lot of weight is the nearest thing there is to a short cut in executive job-hunting.

Bernard Haldane, who has spent a lifetime in job counseling, goes so far as to say that personal recommendations account for as much as 80 per cent of the top-level positions awarded to men outside the company involved. Not every employment expert may agree with the percentage figure, but no dissenting voice is raised to the principle that your best chance—not the only one, mind you, but the very best—lies in mobilizing the support of a big wheel in industry. And the bigger, the better.

Mr. Haldane wisely recommends that the executive job hunter give priority to lining up such personal recommendations which, he warns, are not to be confused with "pull." An outstanding recommendation will get you in touch with the employer who has, or someday may have, the kind of a job you want. After that, it is up to you to make the final sale. The important thing is that with a strong recommendation you have a much better chance of interviewing the *right* man. So treasure your friends; friendship paves the road that leads to better jobs!

All your friends may be helpful to you, but the most valuable ones in a job hunt are those high enough up the ladder to be able to hire you, if they have an opening, and to put in a good word for you with other employers when their own doors are closed.

In all probability you will have to rely on a mere handful of top-level contacts unless you are one of those rare individuals who is on intimate terms with many important men who admire you because of your business capacity and not because you make a good fourth at bridge. A business leader cannot afford to recommend people he does not know very well, even if he has heard they are smart executives, nor can he be expected to endorse those he may be well acquainted with but with whose management capacity he is not familiar. It is a common failing to know important people better than they know you, which is another way of saying that it is a waste of time to seek a recommendation from anyone who is not already sold on your capability.

After you have pondered the matter thoroughly you probably will do some trimming on your list of important contacts. Do not fret if you wind up with only a few names. One good one may be all you need to get the kind of job you want.

The men on your final list are the ones you should approach first, and if you have an idea that any of them has an attractive job open, or one in prospect, he (or they) should be contacted first.

Dash right over (with your résumé in your pocket) to apply for the job you have in mind. You should have entree to the top man through your established friendship and will be able to avoid being waylaid by underlings. Talk only to the executive himself, and make your sales pitch directly to him. You may walk out of his office with a new job. It happens.

Unfortunately, it also frequently happens that your best contacts are not potential employers, for one reason or another, and the most you can hope for from them is a good recommendation. You should go after one as energetically as you would go after a job.

But the approach, now. Should you call on them in

person—as you did on those from whom you sought a job? Or should you telephone for an appointment? Or write a letter with a similar request?

Make an Appointment First

Usually it is best not to call in person without an appointment. Even if a man knows you well and is personally fond of you, he will appreciate being allowed to fix the time of an interview. Therefore, you should ask him in advance when you can see him. This may be done by telephone if you are on better than average terms. Otherwise, a letter probably will be better, and a letter always is preferable when you are dealing with a man who may know a good deal about you but does not see you very often.

Your letter should be brief. A polite request for an appointment on a matter of interest to you, coupled with a promise not to take up much of his time, is sufficient. However, there is no harm in putting in a clincher which could take the form of a suggestion that you telephone his secretary in a few days to learn what time would best suit him. A sentence making it plain that you do not intend to ask him for a job is a nice gesture *if* you are convinced that he does not have one. He will not, for instance, if he is a retired president or heads a company or division of some concern which has no place for an executive with your particular talents.

You will get positive replies in short order—if you have approached the right men. Few, if any, will wait for you to telephone a secretary to fix an appointment date. They will write or telephone you with an invitation, which you should promptly acknowledge with a grateful but not sugary acceptance.

You should never try to change the time of an appointment if there is any way at all for you to be there. And it should take some earth-shaking contingency to keep you away. Perhaps the only excusable ground for seeking a change arises when two of your contacts suggest the same time, and this is so rare a coincidence that you should not give it a thought in mapping your plans. You have asked an important man to see you; make it your business to be there when he tells you he will be available.

Once you arrive, be brief, be concise, be specific, and be friendly. You are looking for a new job; so tell him so and tell him why. He will understand. He may even know more about the details of your present company's predicament than you do. You need help—no use beating around the bush on that score—and so you have decided—after some hesitation, you point out—to seek his advice.

If you have promised not to ask him for a job, keep your promise. But he knows you want something; so do not hesitate to say what it is. You want any suggestions he may have about openings, or potential openings, in your field. He will know that field, naturally, or you have no business bothering him in the first place.

Perhaps there are several companies you think you might like to work for. Tell him the names, and ask if he has any ideas about executive employment prospects with any or all of them. Or does he have any thoughts about where a man with your experience might fit in?

You are not putting your friend through an inquisition when you probe politely for all the bona fide information he may be expected to have, or when you seek all the advice he may reasonably be expected to give. You are overstepping the bounds of propriety, though, if you ask him to do things for you that you should do yourself. You are the man looking for a job. The most you have a right to ask is that he help you to

Do Not Ask Too Much

That brings up one of the more common mistakes made by the anxious job hunter; asking for too much too soon. Suppose he tells you he has heard that the ABC Company is enjoying a good year and might have a spot for a man with your background. That is what you came to see him for; so seize the opportunity immediately. Thank him for the information, and ask which of the high executives in ABC he thinks it would be best to approach first.

Do not tell him that for your purposes, the best man is the one with whom he has the most influence. He knows that as well as you do, and that is where he will send you unless he is on good terms with several of the company's top executives. In that case, he will probably discuss the matter with you, and together you will decide where you should make your first contact. The president, perhaps, or maybe the executive vice president. Or the treasurer, if it is in his department that you hope to work.

Get the official's full name and proper title in any case, and try to learn as much about him as you can with a little polite questioning. But beware of making the mistake of asking your friend to clinch a job by urging someone else point-blank to hire you. An introduction is all you are entitled to expect at this stage of the game, and it is foolish to ask for more.

A personal introduction at a specially arranged luncheon would be ideal, but it is a lot to ask. If your friend is willing to go that far, he probably will suggest it himself. If he does not, however, you should settle for a telephone call or a letter. You may get both, but either will do, and either is a good form of recommendation because one important man does not take up another's time suggesting an interview with a nonentity.

The thing for you to do is follow up the introduction

immediately, doing your best to talk yourself into the job and putting your important friend's name at the top of your list of references. He will be delighted to do a convincing sales job for you *after* he learns the man he sent you to is interested enough to seek an opinion. That is the time when an enthusiastic recommendation will do you the most good anyway.

On the other hand, your friend will not be bothered if the job lead does not pan out and, subconsciously at least, he will be grateful to you for not embarrassing him with a request for a favor he would prefer not to grant. He will respond by doing even more for you when a job does materialize. He will also be inclined to get in touch with you at once if he hears of something else that might be of interest.

So do yourself the favor of making the very best use of your top-flight contacts through the simple expedient of requesting the minimum from them. You will get more by asking less. Besides, company chiefs are not likely to be impressed by an executive who has to get someone else to sell him into a job. Clerks may get by with such tactics, but executives should know better.

The sequence, then, is simple, but it is important. Your contact tells you *who* may be worth calling on; you do the calling yourself—making judicious use of your friend's name—and you invite the company to refer to that friend if they want anything more in the way of a recommendation.

In substance, this amounts to asking *only* for what you need, and only *when* you need it. You need suggestions; so you ask for them. Next, you act on the suggestions you get. Finally, you get the employer himself to ask for whatever else may be needed. Put first things first, and do as much as you can yourself with as little reliance on others as possible.

In our hypothetical case you have had the benefit of threefold help from some important executives. Each has given you a lead to a potential opening; he has made an interview possible; and he is prepared to give you his personal recommendation if approached. This will get you past the receptionist, past the personnel department, past the private secretary, and into the *right* man's office. More executive positions are obtained that way than by any other method.

5

EXECUTIVE EMPLOYMENT LEADS

We have stressed the role your important business friends can play in your job search. Now it must be urged just as strongly that you let nothing obscure the importance of pressing your campaign in other directions, and of keeping it up unceasingly until you get the job you are after.

You can always stop looking when you get a position, but you cannot afford to mark time while you are awaiting the outcome of your earlier efforts. Get into locomotion, and stay there until the job becomes a reality instead of just an objective. The best way to get rolling is to throw out a relentless dragnet for *companies* which have such jobs.

Whether a vacancy exists will be discovered in due course. In the meantime, you have to look around until you do find the opening you want. Line up the companies and you automatically narrow your hunt to the area where your quarry is known to exist. Then ransack that territory as you have never ransacked anything before. This is where you will bag your game—that job, that particular, special job in which you can do your best for yourself and for your employer.

A list of job prospects is a living thing. Like a forest of trees, it keeps growing all the time. You, however, must make it grow, and it will be precisely as long and as good as you make it, no more. Face up to the necessity of continually adding to your prospects so long as you are in the market for a job. Carry on the list right up to the day you start to work.

Source Material

Most libraries have valuable source material, and a good place to start is *Dun & Bradstreet's Million Dollar Directory*. This massive volume lists more than twenty thousand American business enterprises which have an indicated net worth of $1 million or more. Periodic supplements are published to keep the directory up to date.

Million-dollar companies are the kind that cannot do without executives. This particular directory lists the companies alphabetically, separates them by geographical location, and classifies them by product. High-echelon officers and members of the board of directors are named for each individual concern. Elsewhere in the book is an alphabetical list of top management personnel that identifies each executive by his company, making it possible to learn each man's business connections.

Poor's Register of Corporations, Officers and Directors contains substantially similar information about an even larger number of American companies. *Moody's Industrial Manual* supplies pertinent data about companies in the United States, Canada, and abroad, including more financial statistics. The same company also publishes separate manuals covering banks, financial institutions, and public utilities. Each is an excellent source of information for executives in that particular field.

Well worth consulting also is the *Thomas' Register of American Manufacturers,* which is a four-volume directory of all American manufacturing concerns in every line of business. Many of the firms are small, but often a small company is an excellent executive job prospect.

Various industries and professions publish their own directories. For instance, *McKittrick's Directory of Advertisers* and the *Standard Advertising Register* are worth the attention of every man looking for an executive spot in the advertising field. The *Standard Rate & Data Service* is equally valuable to men interested in the newspaper and magazine field, and the *Literary Market Place* should be consulted by everyone looking for a new job in book-publishing.

Most individual states publish annual industrial directories which are informative and have the additional advantage of covering the territory where you live.

The National Association of Manufacturers, the American Management Association, the Society of Automotive Engineers, the American Engineering Society, and the Association of Consulting Management Engineers are just a few of many organizations from which lists of companies are available. Executives interested in overseas work and international trade will find numerous fine prospects in listings which appear in reports on proceedings of annual conventions of the National Foreign Trade Council.

Select the source books you can get your hands on

the easiest—most libraries carry them, and many also are available in the average bank—and get busy making up a personal list of the concerns you would like to join. Write down the complete name of the company, the appropriate address—many have branches here and there—and the number of employees. The importance of the last point will be dealt with later.

Then study the list of officers, and select the name and title of the *highest* official in each company under whom you would expect to work if you were hired by the firm. It is important that you go to the top at the beginning of your campaign, and it may be that the president is the best man to approach. He is the man you almost always should contact first in applying for a job in a medium- or small-sized firm. With a larger company it may be better to see the vice president in charge of the department you seek to join. If the job materializes you may work for a department manager or a division head, but the man who issues the orders that branch of the firm carries out is the man to be seen at the outset. For example, if you are aiming at a job under the controller, the place to start your solicitation is with the treasurer, who, in most companies, is the controller's superior.

For the sake of convenience, if nothing else, start with *nearby* companies which appear to have positions like the one you want to fill. Such positions may or may not be vacant, and your first objective is to find out where the openings are. The closer the company is to where you live the easier it is for you to visit them, and nothing beats a personal call.

Your prospective field obviously is larger if you live in a big city. In that case it is a good idea to compile as long a *good* list as you can in one or two days. Cull out from it the names that seem to you to be the *best* firms to approach. Plan your schedule so that you can call on the highest appropriate executive in each one as soon as possible. Send your résumé to the others, with a brief letter requesting an interview.

Suppose your initial list contains twenty names and you can call on five of the companies fairly soon. While you are talking to them your résumé will be telling your story to the other fifteen. Consequently, you cover a broader territory in a shorter period of time.

Repeat this procedure endlessly. Call in person when and where circumstances permit; write a letter when time or distance run against you. An employed executive lacks the opportunity for as many personal visits as the unemployed man and must, therefore, rely on his résumé to serve as proxy for him. In any case, go there if you can; send a résumé if you cannot. That is the foundation of successful job-hunting.

Does that sound like a discouragingly detailed project? Do not let it get you down. Good jobs do not go begging for applicants. The mountain will not come to you; so you must go to the mountain—if the two of you ever are to get together. In your case there are many mountains, unless your particular talents are so unique that only a few employers could possibly have any use for you. Be thankful if that is true; such jobs are scarce, but even scarcer is the competition.

Regardless of the competition, or the absence of it, the odds are heavily in favor of your having to do some hard work before your job has been successfully tracked down. It will not be easy, and you may be tempted to palm the onerous details off on someone else. Yet, even if you have both the inclination and the financial means to hire others to campaign for you, there still looms up the specter of the job interview. No one can pinch hit for you there. It is like a cough or a sneeze; you have to do it yourself; so you might as well do the whole thing.

Experts may prepare an inspiring résumé for you, but no better than you can write if you but concentrate on the subject which you know better than anyone else because that subject is you. Of course, others may compile lists of companies for you—but can you be certain they include *all* the firms you want to contact? And that they do not include a lot of dead wood? Your best defense against such risks is to prepare the list yourself.

Perhaps others can refer you to a prospective employer, and put in a good word for you. An offer like that should be seized upon immediately. Take advantage of everything others can do for you better than you can do yourself, but if you do not get the job—or it is slow in crystallizing—do not slow down for a moment in campaigning in other directions. Press ahead as energetically as you can, using all *practical* channels that may possibly lead to employment.

Being practical about your job hunt means concentrating on companies where you think you have the best chance of getting a job. Sending copies of your résumé out at random is not the way to get ahead. You must select the prospects, which means you have to sit down with a good source directory, a writing pad, a pen or a pencil—and unlimited patience.

Painstakingly analyze the companies, one by one, just as you analyzed your personal qualifications when you were preparing your résumé. Be selective—at least in the beginning. The time may come when you will have to be less particular—probably it will not—but until you *have* to saturate the market, don't. Right now, when you are just getting started, aim at the most promising targets.

Read Help-wanted Columns

Important as preparing this list is, there are other things you should do in prosecuting your job hunt. Reading the "help wanted" advertisements is a good example. Go over the columns in every available newspaper and trade publication. Study them, item by item and word by word. *The New York Times,* especially the Sunday edition, and the *Wall Street Journal,* are among the more favored advertising media for executive-seeking employers.

Answer *every* advertisement that seems to offer interesting possibilities. Get your résumé in the mail immediately, but resign yourself to the fact that a job often is less attractive than the ad made it appear. More often than that, you will appear less desirable to the employer than you think you are. However, you do not have to accept a job you do not like, and you will not be offered one the employer thinks you cannot fill, so do not go overboard in harsh prejudgment. Just be careful. Shun advertised jobs you do not want or obviously cannot fill; apply for all the rest.

Register with Employment Agencies

Employment agencies, too, have a definite place in your campaign. Not just any agency, of course, but every agency which caters to executives in your profession. Big cities have many such agencies. Register with them all, and keep going back—at least once a week—just as any good salesman keeps calling regularly on potential customers to insure that he gets the order when buying time arrives.

Making the rounds of employment agencies is not exactly stimulating, and you must fortify yourself against the possibility of running into a chilly reception in a good many of them. Nevertheless, you must keep going back to every one that accepts your application because that is the only way to keep your application in their *active* file. Treat it as something you have to do for your own good, such as a periodic visit to the dentist. You will learn a lot about human nature, if nothing else. And you may get a worthwhile job interview.

Most employment agencies operate with a minimum staff while striving to corral the maximum number of clients. Therefore, you will probably have to wait before you can talk with anyone, but in the interim you can fill out an application blank. This will call for a record of the jobs you have held, and the agency will not accept a chronological résumé in its place. Attach one to it anyway, because your résumé contains a sales pitch the employment form lacks.

You will also have to supply routine biographical data and state the salary you wish to receive. This figure is as important to the agency as it is to you; so be sure to have in mind how much you want. Some agencies ask that you name the salary you seek and the *minimum* you will accept. Supply that information, but be sure to decide ahead of time precisely what those figures are. You may pull a boner if you jot something down on the spur of the moment.

Your age may provoke some preliminary questions from the receptionist. It is almost certain to if the agency does not make a practice of catering to mature executives. Answer them politely and factually, but do not volunteer any explanations. Thank the receptionist and leave if you are told the agency cannot do anything for you. Fill out the blank and wait your turn if you are told you will have to speak to one of the interviewers.

When your turn finally comes, stick to facts. Put your best foot forward but do not try to force yourself on anyone. Do not argue if you are told your age is against you. And do not be surprised if the interviewer is a woman. The distaff side predominates in the employment agency business.

Most agencies dealing in executive placement, either exclusively or in conjunction with other jobs, will accept you unless your salary is markedly higher than the maximum they are accustomed to handling. Those willing to see what they can do for you will ask you to sign a contract. This binds you to pay their fee if they get a job for you, and it also requires that you notify them immediately if you get a job through other sources. Sign it and leave, but make a point of calling on them in person at least once a week thereafter.

Executive Recruiters

Contacting so-called executive recruiters comes next. You can obtain lists of such firms from a number of business and professional associations on request. Two valuable sources are the American Management Association, 1515 Broadway, and the Association of Consulting Management Engineers, 347 Madison Avenue, both in New York City. Write to whichever organization you select, asking for their list and enclosing a stamped, self-addressed envelope.

In recent years various individuals and agencies have begun to sell lists of executive recruiting concerns for a dollar or two. Their advertisements usually appear in the larger newspapers, and you may or may not wish to buy one. Most of the names can be gotten free, however.

A typical list contains each firm's name and address, its occupation specialty (if any), the minimum salary involved (most of them will not consider a man seeking less than $10,000, and many have a much higher minimum), a note saying whether it is willing to review résumés, and a final word about whether it will grant interviews before it invites them.

The occupational specialty may be something like "sales executives," or "marketing specialists," or "electronic research," or it may be a broad term such as "senior executives." Consider only those in your employment field and salary range. Call in person on as many as possible of the firms which agree to interviews. Send your résumé to the others (provided they will review résumés, of course), even if they are in distant cities. Successful recruiters usually cover a broad territory. Many operate on a nationwide scale.

Executive recruiters charge a fee—and a fat one, at that—if they place you in a position conforming to your specifications. However, in many cases the fee is paid by the employer. You pay it only if the employer does not.

Most executive recruiting offices also are management consultants, and they do a lot more than hunt for a good executive when a client needs one. Consequently, they will not charge you anything unless they line up a job for you with a client firm which will not make the payment itself. Neither are they apt to exert themselves in your behalf unless and until a client puts in a call for someone with your qualifications and background. They do not look for jobs; they look for an executive when a job is open. You gain nothing by repeated calls; so do not pester them. Do remind them that you still are available if you have not gotten a post in three or four months.

Executive recruiters fill many good jobs, but the more candid ones will admit that the number of *unemployed* executives they place hovers around the zero mark. There is a good reason. The recruiter is leading with his chin when he recommends an executive who is out of work. There may be the most plausible excuse in the world for your current idleness; nevertheless, the fact remains that you are idle. The recruiter will have to explain why you are not working before he can get the client to listen to an exposition of your talents. It is much easier to get a receptive hearing when he can offer someone presently working. Every employer likes to think he is getting a bargain, and a man who has lost a job just does not look like one.

And there are other reasons for reluctance to go to bat for an unemployed executive, less creditable ones, perhaps, but valid nonetheless. Obviously, the idle executive is making a strong pitch for himself. Quite possibly, he already has tackled the recruiter's client, in person or by mail. However, he has not sold himself or the job would be filled. The recruiter will be in the unhappy position of trying to unload a warmed-over prospect if he proposes someone who has been rejected. Mind you, he will not know for certain that the application has been made, but discretion dictates that he not risk such a possibility.

Then there is the matter of his fee. If the employer is paying it, he expects the recruiter to comb the employment field and pick up just the right man: a man who is proving he can fill the new job by performing admirably in a similar one at that very moment. The fee-paying employer may feel he has been taken if he is offered an unemployed man whom he could have hired himself without paying anyone to dig up the applicant.

Another, and possibly a minor, angle may enter into the case. The recruiter who transplants an executive from one employer to another may be retained to find a replacement for the first company. That gives him a chance at two fees instead of just one.

Viewed from any angle, your best and probably your only chance to get a job through executive recruiters is by contacting them while you are still working. Still, there is no harm in registering anyway, and if you do, try to wangle as many personal interviews as possible. Recruiters know the field, and most of them are able and willing to give you genuinely helpful advice. Listen to their suggestions, and put them into practice.

Executive Search Firms

At the opposite end of the pole from the executive recruiter is the "executive search firm" whose clients are men looking for executive jobs. Some of them try to work both sides of the street, and a few succeed, but by and large they make their money hunting jobs for men who want them—and charging for this service. Note these differences: First, the recruiter has the job and seeks the man, whereas the searcher has the man and seeks the job; and, second, the recruiter does not charge you anything until he places you in a job (and not even then if the employer pays), whereas the searcher collects a fee at the outset.

The job-search agency writes your résumé and it contacts prospective employers for you, by mail and by telephone. It also professes to know more about where good jobs are than you do, and maybe it does. The more imposing ones run you through a series of psychological tests, often lasting an entire day, intended to uncover your most promising talents.

Retainers, payable in advance, usually run from $500 to $1,000, depending on your salary bracket. Their placement commissions also are high, and there is less chance that the employer will assume that expense. However, some search firms do let you deduct your retainer from the final placement commission.

Employers tend to place more reliance on executive recruiters, because they have to screen candidates thoroughly in self-defense. Screening also is a part of the search firm's routine, but it is less likely to reject an applicant, because a retainer is lost every time it does.

The principal advantage search firms can offer is the third-party approach. They can brag about you all over the place, whereas you are apt to be somewhat diffident in puffing yourself. Ordinary employment agencies can do that much, however, and you do not have to pay them anything until they get you a job. The search firm, of course, is being well compensated for what it does.

Nevertheless, it is worthwhile to call on one or two

when you have time, just to hear their sales talk. You can get their names from the newspapers—they advertise where employment agencies do—and you may learn something from the interviews that will improve your own sales effort.

Nine times out of ten you will be kept waiting a few minutes in an anteroom which will be plentifully supplied with magazines and the firm's promotional material. Pass the magazines by and read their stuff, which probably will include examples of the résumés they write. Study these carefully, noting both the text and the arrangement. You may pick up an idea or two, but do not be surprised if you find them no better than the one you have already written. Some searchers have a mania for jamming the whole story onto a single page, and praise themselves for it at every opportunity. That makes pretty heavy reading if an executive's background is properly covered. Everything is there but the white space that makes a résumé easy to digest.

On the other hand, some executive search firms turn out excellent résumés; as good as you can write yourself. Their letters also are good, and so is their telephone technique. However, there is a lot to be said in favor of saving your money and depending on your own efforts for a while. Do not be in a rush to put your job-hunting campaign in the hands of someone who charges you in advance for everything he does.

Executive Job Counselors

Along with the advertisements of executive recruiters and executive search firms you will see those of "executive job counselors," who make a business of teaching you how to become a do-it-yourself job hunter. Their educational contributions also command a fee. You can expect to pay at least $500 for their services.

As their title implies, they go in heavily for advice-giving and the reputable ones are capable of offering many worthwhile suggestions. Among other things they will provide excellent pointers on résumé writing —some will even draft one for you—and they are skilled at drafting letters and grooming executives on proper behavior during interviews.

If you sign a contract you will be called upon to supply complete biographical data—far more than just your employment and educational record—and you probably will be given at least one aptitude test. You also will be put through some psychological quizzes, and what you say and write will be studied to determine the type of job you can best fill. If it does not closely match your own job objective, someone has wasted a lot of time. Fortunately, drastic changes are seldom recommended.

Some job counselors are executive search firms in disguise. Others disclaim any job-search intent, but usually add that they are often called upon to recommend someone for an executive position and, naturally, look first to their own list of clients. They will cut you in on any such benefits that may arise, they assure you, when you become a part of their clientele.

In the meantime, if you sign up you will be booked for regular interviews in which you report your progress, or the lack of it, and you also will have the privilege of contacting the counselor assigned to handle your case whenever you feel in need of advice.

A client who is still employed may be counseled to hang onto his job if humanly possible or, failing that, to concentrate on trying to arrange for a transfer to some other position within his employer's firm. He may, and often does, get worthwhile suggestions about the best approach to make, the type of job to aim at, and what kind of a proposition to advance to his current boss.

Some job-counseling contracts bind you to pay an

additional commission your increased annual rate of earnings during the term of your agreement. This commission is payable whether you improve your status with your present employer or get a better-paying job somewhere else. In a sense, this may be largely sales talk designed to encourage you to take the plunge by intimating that you will be on the threshold of improved earning capacity as soon as you retain the counselor's services.

The contract may not contain such a provision. At other times it may be waived with considerable ostentation. Whether a pointed waiver means your prospects for bettering your employment situation are remote is something to deduce for yourself.

The decision whether to invest your time and money in a job counselor also is yours to make. As in the case of the executive search firm, you are not likely to hurt yourself if you defer such an expenditure until you have given your own personally conducted job-hunting campaign a fair trial.

Summary

To summarize the situation thus far, you should register with appropriate employment agencies and with suitable executive recruiters because they already have contacts you are still trying to develop. They may be able to shorten your job hunt, and the time saved could be worth more than their commission. Besides, it will not cost you anything until you get the job, and you may not have to pay the recruiter even then.

Executive search firms and job counselors come under the heading of luxuries—nice to have, maybe, but not to be indulged in until essentials have first been taken care of. Unless you have money to burn, you might as well go slow about spending more than necessary before you are enjoying satisfactory payroll arrangements.

The expenses can be substantial in any case; the saving grace of agencies that do not charge a retainer is that their services are C.O.D. By the time they submit a bill, you are earning the money to pay them.

Even states which rigidly limit employment agency commissions seldom put a ceiling on levies against jobs paying more than $10,000 a year. Five per cent of the gross annual salary is rock bottom. It is more likely to be 10 per cent, and may run higher if you pass the $20,000 mark. Search firms charge about what the more expensive employment agencies collect, and executive recruiters are the most costly of all.

Services of the U.S. Employment Service and the various state employment offices are available without charge, but they are lamentably unsuccessful in placing executives. No matter how you look at it, you are still your own best agent.

6

THE JOB INTERVIEW

All your efforts at résumé writing, contacting important friends, and lining up companies you would like to work for are aimed primarily at gaining interviews. A job is the ultimate goal, but interviews *always* precede the actual hiring process. Consequently, the way you handle yourself while talking to a prospective employer is tremendously important.

"The interview is the place where the job is won or lost," says Alvin L. Grant, director of placement for Pace College in New York City. "Never be perfunctory about it." Mark his words because your professional future may depend on your coming through when the chips are down—and they are down when you face a prospective employer across his desk.

Some jobs are better than others, but it is hard to say that any one job interview is *less* important than another. You are virtually on trial every time, and you must aim for a victory in each one. Take the view that this is the interview that you must negotiate successfully. Imagine that you are the manager of a baseball team facing the final and deciding game in the World Series. Before the day is over you will either head the champions or the also-rans. Forget about tomorrow, or next week, or next year. Concentrate on today's game, and only today's game.

A job interview, of course, is much more serious than a ball game, but there is a resemblance, not the least similarity being that you have to plan in advance for both. The first thing to do prior to an interview is to bone up on the company. Find out exactly what it does, where it operates, how many branches or subsidiaries it has, whether it is expanding at home or abroad, what processes it specializes in, how it merchandises its product, where it stands in comparison with its competitors, and what progress it has made in the industry over the past five or six years.

Do your best to learn something, as well, about the man who will interview you. This will be easy if the meeting is the result of an introduction by one of your important friends. Your contact knows the man pretty well and can tell you about the company officer's personality, his likes and his dislikes, his history in the concern (and in other firms if he is a relative newcomer), his educational background, where he lives, and exactly what part he plays in the organizational setup.

Unfortunately, personal information like that often is hard to get when you are approaching a prospect through your own efforts or as a result of an advertise-

ment, but do not let that discourage you. A little research will tell you a great deal about the company,
and that is the most important thing. You can do without intimate knowledge of the official himself if you
have to, but try to learn something anyway. You can
always refer to *Who's Who,* where he may be listed.

Do not be late for an interview under any circumstances, but do not barge in too early either. If you
arrive well ahead of time, keep out of sight until it is
appropriate to make your appearance. Then walk in
with the air that befits you, which is the attitude of
an executive on his way to an important meeting with
another executive.

The man you are about to see has something you
want—a job—and you have something he wants—executive talent. The two of you could make a fine team,
and there is an excellent chance that you will, provided
you convince him how valuable you can be to him and
his company.

So much for that. You are an executive, not a
trainee, and you learned long ago that you have to
justify the salary you expect to collect. Your contention
is that an investment in you will bring a substantial return to the investor. In offering your services you are
selling a "blue chip," not a speculation; but, of course,
you will have to substantiate your claims.

Define the Job You Are After

Confidence in yourself is essential, and so is a definite
plan of approach. You are after a job, and you must define that job so that the employer will understand precisely what is on your mind. It has been said that in the
average interview, you have perhaps a maximum of
thirty seconds in which to capture the attention of your
prospect. You can do it if you are unmistakably clear
about your job objective immediately, and from then
on the company officer will follow everything you say

if you handle yourself properly. On the other hand, his mind is bound to wander if you cite three or four jobs you can fill and leave it up to him to decide which should be chosen.

Remember that a *single* job objective is essential to your *initial* sales pitch because you can always sell one thing at a time better than you can sell several. It does not rule out other jobs, however, and if the firm has any which you could fill, this probably will come out during the interview. Then is the time to switch tactics subtly, and to sell yourself on the new one, which might be better anyway.

A single job objective is defined with reference to the company involved in the interview. You may have a totally different goal with another firm, and in your over-all program it is not unlikely that you will be prepared to handle three or four different types of executive activity. Nevertheless, you must always start out with *one* proposal Say exactly what you want, but do *not* mention anything else that you would decline. Be affirmative all the way, but leave the door open for a counterproposition which may be offered.

When you are answering an advertisement or have been referred to a company about a specific opening, your task is easier because you know the type of work involved and are aware that it would be foolish to talk about anything else unless the company official tells you they have other jobs available. You may run into complications, however, when you are invited to an interview without knowing exactly what opening, if any, may exist. You want to join the company, but you must do more than just say that; you must tell in what capacity you want to join *and what you can do for the firm* if you get the job.

Will your interviewer reply that he is sorry but they do not have that kind of work in his company? He certainly will not unless you have bungled the job of investigating the firm. He may say they do not have an opening in your particular field at the moment, but that is your cue to put yourself in line when a vacancy does occur. There must be prospects or there would be no interview. Make the most of the opportunity.

That involves matching your experience, along with your personality, your age, and your health, with the employer's requirements. You can do best by stressing the areas in which you know you can make significant contributions to the company, and you can help yourself along in that direction by demonstrating a knowledge of the functions, the responsibilities, and the authority that go with the job you expect to fill.

When you get down to the solid business of the interview you may find the company man wants to do most of the talking. That is his privilege; so let him have his own way. If he fires questions at you, field each one promptly, directly, factually—and briefly. He can afford to ramble on and on—he probably will not, incidentally—but you cannot. Besides, a concise answer has the effect of putting the next move up to him without any obvious maneuver on your part, which is exactly what you want. The more he talks, the more you learn and the better position you are in to answer his queries.

What the interviewer says can give you some good leads; so take advantage of them. As he talks, the things he considers most important will take shape. Bear down hard on your own qualifications in the line closest to his thoughts. You may be surprised to learn, through him, that the single job objective you walked in with has less attraction than other possibilities for which you are equally qualified.

Be flexible. Avoid putting yourself in a strait jacket early in the interview. You had a particular job in mind, but one of the things that led you to seek an interview in the first place was the desire to join a com-

pany with broad opportunities for a go-getting executive. When the interviewer pinpoints some of those
opportunities you should seize upon each opening,
meanwhile giving him a silent vote of thanks for pav-
ing the way.

You may be subjected to a searching inquisition.
That is to be expected; so take it in stride. If a question
is ambiguous or difficult to understand or seemingly
irrelevant, do not tell him so. Get it cleared up but not,
for heaven's sake, by a "How's-that-again?" approach.

Above all, do not risk making a guess about what the
man is driving at. If you are in doubt, get it straight
before you try to state your position. A counterquestion is better than a hazy answer, but something like
"What do you mean?" is not a counterquestion. "Do
you mean thus-and-so?" is better, and if that is, indeed,
what he does mean, give the answer. If it is not he will
correct you—which means he is also correcting himself,
but he does not know it and thus will not be offended
—and then you answer the corrected question.

The answers you give and, for that matter, almost
everything you say may draw an objection, and it is up
to you to meet it head on, without subterfuge and without delay.

Meet every such point by clarification, not by con-
tradiction. He may be wrong but he is the boss—at least
the boss of the interview if not yet of you—and your
role is to clear up his misconception by discreetly introducing more facts that bolster your interpretation without deprecating his.

In any case, be sure you answer thoughtfully and
deliberately, but not too slowly. To give the impression
that you are mentally groping for something to say can
be as damaging as firing back off-the-cuff answers that
may stamp you as a man who cannot think things out.

Types of Questions to Expect

Job counselors often remind men bound for an interview that they must be prepared for two types of questions: Those which come from a line operator—the man you will most likely work for, for example—and those which come from a staff-recruiting specialist such as the personnel director.

The line operator will probably get right down to business. Your qualifications, or the lack of them, will be exposed in almost no time, and he will need little convincing either way, because he is an expert. Therefore, having satisfied himself that you do know what you are talking about, he will concentrate on the specific dimensions of the job and on how you fit them. That is the ideal situation, because you will be dealing with a man who talks the same language. He will grasp the points you make as readily as you understand the questions he asks.

The staff expert may be equally capable of judging your exact skills, and if he is, so much the better. The chances are, though, that he will not, unless you, by a coincidence, are in the same line. He will, however, be able to size up your experience and personality, and he will undoubtedly compare you with other candidates for the job.

Furthermore, since he is supposed to get the best man possible, he will try to uncover your strong points *and* your weak ones. You can expect him to be thorough because, in a sense, his own job depends on you. He rates higher in the company every time he recommends a good man.

As the staff interviewer talks to you he will silently ask himself how much you are worth to his company and how good you can make him look. He must get a satisfactory answer to both questions or you will not get past him, and that is important because he stands *between* you and the company executive you will work for if you are hired.

You cannot afford to talk down to the staff interviewer, even if he is a second-rater. Most of the time he will not be, but good, bad, or indifferent, he holds a key position; so behave accordingly. Be careful not to belittle any of his questions. Let him have the satisfaction of thinking you do not realize he is not the executive he pretends to be, and make the very best presentation of yourself that lies within your power. If you play the game the way you should, an interview with the top-level line operator will follow in due course, and there is where you will get a final yes-or-no answer.

As a general rule it is advisable to introduce your strong points in a subtle, unostentatious way. Even if you are an executive with uncommon qualifications which have enabled you to achieve a unique record, you must be careful how you talk about them. Otherwise, you will be written off as a conceited braggart. On the other hand, you must conduct yourself as one successful man meeting another, and that invariably requires two or three examples of past achievements. Furnish them unhesitatingly, but discreetly, at the *appropriate* moment. This may come early in the interview or it may come late. Knowing *when* to talk about yourself is just as important as knowing *how*.

In almost every interview you have to time your presentation to fit in with the company official's remarks, and one of the pitfalls often encountered is the interviewer who gives you a free rein. Be on your guard whenever a prospective employer invites you to "talk about yourself," and then sits back in his chair with a display of amiable interest in whatever you may care to say.

Such a situation can be dangerous. Protect yourself against making a false step. Narrow the conversation down to something tangible, which will not be difficult if you have studied the company in advance. Utilize the knowledge you have gained by referring at once to some phase of the company's activity which resembles work you have handled successfully, and continue with a concise description of what you did in a parallel situation.

A somewhat more timid response but one that is not without merit involves giving the interviewer several alternatives. You can ask, for example, if he would prefer that you start with your background in such-and-such a line, or your responsibilities in the head office (or a branch or subsidiary), or your experience in dealing with militant labor unions.

Do not make the mistake of asking, "Where would you like me to start?" That is as vague as his invitation. Give him something to think about and perhaps he will pick up one of your suggestions and tell you to fill in the details. That is fine; just proceed immediately along those lines, with emphasis on some noteworthy accomplishment in that connection. On the other hand, he may invite you to make your own choice, in which case, obviously, you describe the role in which you achieved your *greatest* success.

Whatever line you take, pound your point home in that particular field and tie it in with what you would expect to do along similar lines in the interviewer's company. Then pause long enough to give him a chance to pick up the conversation. He may do it by volunteering some comment of his own or by asking another question.

What you must especially guard against is wasting time on biographical data of no particular importance to the prospective job, on the one hand, and dissipating your ammunition by covering too many phases of your career, on the other. You do not want to let yourself be inveigled into discharging a shotgun blast when you really should be firing a bullet.

The employer may have done this deliberately—it is a good way to test a man's executive capacity—or he may have just intended to be agreeable. It is not the intent that is important, however; it is the necessity of concentrating your fire on the target. If you talk too long about too many features about yourself, you may wind up sounding like a man who has made a stab at all sorts of things without really mastering anything.

Tips on Interview Technique

Here are some pointers that experts give for *all* interviews:

Be persuasive, not argumentative. If you argue you will probably talk yourself *out* of consideration for the job you are trying to talk yourself into.

Do not be offensive, even if you think the interviewer is. He may just be the brusque type, but no matter what he is you cannot afford to lose your temper. You are an executive, remember.

Personalities should be left out of interviews, except for the customary character references. There is no excuse at all for derogatory personal references about anyone. You will sound like a sorehead if you reflect on present or former employers—or on almost anyone else, for that matter—and if you are goaded into contemplating a snappy retort to the interviewer himself, you have probably applied to the wrong company.

Name-dropping is a common fault. You may be on cordial terms with some of the most important people in town, but limit them to your reference list. Indiscreet mention of big names seldom pleases anyone. The prospective employer probably is not much interested in who you know anyway; he will be impressed, however, when he learns that the important people you referred him to do know you, and like you.

Running down your present job or employer is fatal. If they are no good, what good are you? You can look for a change without being critical. Say that the job you have is a fine one, just the thing for a good man, but not up to your standards under existing conditions. Or—and you must admit this if it is the reason for your job hunt—that merger, or acquisition, or loss of the big government contract means the post you occupy will be dissolved.

Preparing for Hard Questions

You have to know the product you are selling, and even though the product is you and your own background, it is surprisingly easy to fall down on the sales pitch. So prepare in advance for questions like these:

Why did you leave your last job (or are you leaving your present one)? As mentioned above there is only one answer; tell the truth.

What is the state of your health? You have to answer that one truthfully but, if possible, undamagingly. You are in middle age, so the prospective employer has a right to question your physical capacity.

What do you have to offer our company?

Could you work for a younger man?

What is your strongest quality as an executive?

How do you get along with your present employer (or how did you with your last boss)?

What type of work do you like to do best? Least?

All such questions are easily answered if they have been thought out, but they may be hard to handle if you are caught by surprise. Be prepared for queries along those lines.

What you offer the company is embodied in your sales pitch, or should be, so spread yourself out.

Of course you can work for a younger man. (At your age, you are in a hell of a fix if you can't, but keep that to yourself.)

Get some advice about that "strongest executive quality" of yours. Your wife probably has ideas. So have other relatives. Find out what they think, and also go in for self-analysis. Do the same for your weakest qualities.

Either you get along with your boss, or you do not, but assume that you do unless it is common knowledge that you have had a big fight. Be the most surprised man in town if there is a hint anywhere from any source that you do not work hand-in-glove with the man who gives you orders. Be emphatic about this because you will be tabbed as a trouble-maker if you do not, and that is one label it is almost impossible for an executive ever to rub off.

You like your employer. You enjoy working for him, and you have learned a lot from him. That is your side of the story. If there is another version, let someone else tell it.

You alone know what kind of work you like and dislike. If the potential employer wants to know, tell him, but do not dwell on the disliking part. That is negative; your emphasis on the positive is what will get you a job.

All of this calls for considerable talking on your part so be careful not to get yourself started on a flow of conversation you may forget to turn off. A yen for talking is a common failing in middle age. You have seen more and done more than your younger associates; so you have more to talk about. Just remember that it is easy to ramble on and on in a long exposition of something that interests you tremendously—especially if it is about some exploit or experience of your own—but is of dubious importance to the man you hope will hire you.

Salary

He is not likely to ask you anything personal, but he will have other questions, including some you would probably just as soon not have to answer. One of the most irksome—a perennial bane to all job hunters on the management level—is: "What salary do you expect?"

You will not always run into this, but often you will, and it can be a headache, especially if it comes early in the interview. Most job counselors advise delaying the answer as long as possible, unless it comes near the end of your meeting. In that case, of course, there is no bona fide excuse for dodging it any longer.

The advantage of putting off a salary declaration until other details of the job have been threshed out is that the delay gives you a fill-in on the entire scope of the position itself, including the present and potential responsibilities involved and the opportunity for advancement.

Until those job features have been thoroughly covered, any salary proposal on your part would be based on little more than your personal desire for a certain sum of money. That is important to you, of course, but it has no justifiable place in the interview. Probably you will always secretly want more than you know you will get, but discussing salary should be deferred until the employer decides that you are qualified for the job and you consider the position attractive.

Therefore, feel free to sidestep the salary question that comes early in an interview, but be diplomatic. It is not smart to say, "Let's take that up later," or words to that effect. A better way is to suggest that more details about the position, and your ability to handle them, be discussed so that you will both know what you can do for the company. Then deftly lead into a discussion of exactly what the post entails.

In your sales pitch, as well as in your answers to questions thrown at you, place your main emphasis on your desire to fit into a job where you can exercise your talents to the best advantage of your employer and yourself. You may be desperate to get on a payroll, but that is the last thing to admit. The interviewer knows you expect to get an executive's salary for executive work, and if the job is worthy of your attention you are entitled to get the specifications before you name a price.

Sooner or later, of course, the salary question has to come up, and in many cases the employer will already have decided the maximum he will pay. If a good man can be gotten for less, however, few companies will let the opportunity escape. So you may have to declare your intentions.

Bernard Haldane says a good way to proceed is to negotiate for *future* salary wherever possible, and leave the starting salary figure to be named by the interviewer. A $15,000 man might say, "This sounds like something that would give me the opportunity to prove I am worth $18,000 or so in three to five years. With such an opportunity of course I'm willing to leave the starting salary to your good judgment. About how much were you thinking of paying?"

Such an approach labels you a future $18,000 man who can be obtained for much less now, and it helps avoid a direct answer to the question. It also politely tosses the starting salary question back in the interviewer's lap.

You can also fish around for more information—to which you are entitled—by asking if there are any stock options attached to the job, or if profit-sharing is practiced by the company, or if there is a bonus plan.

Another question advocated by Mr. Haldane is, "Would you say that my record makes me worth $15,000 in salary?"

Or you may come out with a point-blank query of your own, such as "What is the salary range for the position you have in mind?" The importance of the word *range* will not be missed by the interviewer. It conveys the thought that you do not insist on starting at the top if there is room for advancement. You expect to grow with the job, and to graduate to a better one so that the employer will get an increasingly higher return on his increasing investment in your talents.

You may read too much or you may read too little into the interviewer's salary questions, but in answering all of them you have to use discretion. Tailor your comments to fit the immediate situation. Undoubtedly you have a salary floor below which you will not work. Do not disclose it, however, unless such a declaration is absolutely unavoidable. Neither is it smart to admit that you have a ceiling on your ambitions. You want to make increasingly valuable contributions to the firm; stress that fact without adding that you expect appropriate remuneration in return. The interviewer understands that much without being told.

If you have not told him, he may ask what you expect to be doing five years from now. And ten. And what annual income would satisfy you then. Tell him the truth as you see it, but keep salaries on the floor level—never the ceiling. And stress what you expect to be *worth* to him. Do not let a word slip out that may indicate you will *insist* that he pay you a certain figure at some future date. You want to be worth so much to him that he will gladly pay it to keep you. Let it go at that.

Are You Overqualified?

Here is another question that is a real stickler, but one that is forever cropping up when a middle-aged executive is being interviewed. Aren't you "overqualified" or "too experienced" for this job?

You have to tread warily in dealing with this one. Remind the questioner that a strong company needs a strong man in every important job, and capitalize on the very objection he has voiced. Stress your qualifications as contrasted with those of a less experienced man—which also means a younger man—and bring out discreetly that experienced executives are at a premium today as never before.

An executive with your qualifications needs much less time to get ahead in the job. Your employer will start earning a return on his investment in you faster because you have *more* than is required instead of less. You have to get acclimated in a new job; everyone does. But there are many things you will not have to be taught because you already know them. There is no substitute for experience, and everything you already know represents a tangible asset the company will acquire when it hires you.

There will be many questions asked in most interviews, and all must be answered. You may delay some of them, but never avoid them. "Delay" does not mean "stall." You delay only to get necessary information, and you then answer on the basis of that information. Be sure, of course, that you have answered every question before the interview comes to an end.

Above all, sell yourself. You should not have to be told how important that is, but many middle-aged executives do have to be reminded that personal downgrading can be disastrous. Note this comment by the Committee on Employment of Mature Workers of the National Association of Manufacturers:

Too frequently the mature job seeker is his own stumbling block. Instead of accenting his ability and skills when he applies for a job, he sometimes magnifies the matter of his age. And if he does not get the position, he often feels sure he is rejected because of his age, never realizing that he might have fallen short of the job requirements.

Here are some of the things the NAM committee urges you to do:

Stress your qualifications for the job. Recount experience you have had which fits you for the job. Talk and think, as far as possible, about the future rather than the past. Emphasize your stability and attendance record. Take a record of your former work connections with you to the interview. Be confident, be respectful (without being servile), and be optimistic. Make a point of your flexibility, your resilience, and your readiness to learn.

Among the committee's "Don'ts" are these:

Don't keep stressing your need for a job.

Don't cringe or beg for consideration.

Don't discuss past experience which has no application to the job.

Don't apologize for your age.

Don't display "cocksureness."

Don't be a "know-it-all" or person who cannot take instructions.

There are many more "do's" and "don'ts" which a moment's reflection will bring home to the earnest executive. Rules of etiquette loom large among them. You must be tidy, well-groomed, and presentable. You must not be nervous, fidgety, or impatient. You must be on time, but you must not fret if the interviewer is late.

There are some other elementary but important points to bear in mind. Let the interviewer invite you to be seated before you look around to see where the chairs are. Do not offer to shake hands—that is the interviewer's prerogative—but respond with a friendly businesslike handclasp if he extends the invitation.

Never walk into an interview with a cigarette, cigar, or pipe in your mouth. Do not smoke during the interview unless invited to, and even then it is usually better to refrain. Sit upright in your chair, without slouching or slumping. Do not twiddle your thumbs or drum your fingers. Speak clearly, with no mumbling or groping for words. School yourself to avoid "er's" and "uh's" and heavy breathing.

Look at the interviewer unless he is interrupted by a telephone call or the entry of a subordinate. Then it is a mark of politeness to glance away. While either of you is talking, though, it is downright amateurish to stare at the ceiling, or at a point on the wall, or out of the window. Keep your attention on the business at hand *all* the time.

Everyone who has ever studied employment problems warns the job hunter against hanging around, prolonging an interview when it should be over. When it is time to go—go! And leave briskly; do not shamble off. But it is important to remember that the first interview is seldom the last one. Therefore, make sure that you earn a second interview and that you leave the employer with a favorable impression of you.

Having created that impression, it is wise to lay the groundwork, as unnoticeably as possible, for that second interview, which probably is the one that will determine whether or not you get the job. Ask politely when it will be convenient for you to call again, and you may be invited to drop in next week. Of course if you are told, "Don't call me, I'll call you," you cannot do anything more than thank the interviewer and leave.

A letter of thanks should always be sent after each interview. Everyone is in agreement on that point. It is a matter of elementary courtesy, but it also helps keep your name in the employer's mind. More than that, it gives you an excuse to amplify important points not already covered to your satisfaction, or to correct possible misapprehensions left behind, or to transmit supplemental information that has a bearing on the job. But keep the letter brief in any event, and get it in the mail within twenty-four hours.

By its very definition, the thank-you letter must come *after* the interview. There is a place *in* the interview, however, for other material you want the employer to have and he wants you to give him.

Take with you, without fail, appropriate reports, surveys, and samples of your work to support your job application. You must supply a concise, informative black-and-white record of your outstanding achievements for your own good, and the employer usually will want a list of your employers back to the very starting point. The application blank you may have to fill in will give the skeleton information. Build some real meat around the bones by attaching a chronological résumé.

7

ADVERTISE YOUR AVAILABILITY

Peddling your own wares—executive talent in this case
—automatically puts you in the marketing business, and
nowhere is the maxim "it pays to advertise" more true
than here. A well-written advertisement will make a
fine addition to your direct mail, personal solicitation,
and word-of-mouth campaign.

A position-wanted advertisement may profitably be
placed in a trade publication or in a leading newspaper
—or in both. Your particular profession may or may not
have a trade publication that is a good advertising
medium for executives seeking jobs. Judge all periodicals by the ads they carry.

Executives in less specialized fields may find a newspaper ad will produce better results. Limit yourself to newspapers which carry a substantial number of ads of your type, and place your own in the issue when the most personnel notices appear. That is Sunday for *The New York Times* and Monday for the *Wall Street Journal,* to cite two examples.

A classified ad, which is the cheapest kind, should go in the "Executive Positions Wanted" column or the nearest equivalent; otherwise, your message may be buried in a flock of lesser offerings that could range from file clerks to night watchmen.

A "Position Wanted" classified ad is a thumbnail sketch, when you get right down to it, and if one appears in your résumé it will be an excellent nucleus for your advertisement. So will your straight job objective, with minor variations. If neither packs a real punch, draw up a genuine attention-getter for the newspaper ad; then use it (or a condensed version) to start off a new résumé.

Be sure the ad mentions any important educational assets—an M.B.A. from the Harvard Business School, for instance. Do not say where you live unless such information is pertinent. It might be if you are looking for a European assignment and are already established in Paris. Your willingness to travel or relocate undoubtedly is in your résumé but may not appear in your thumbnail sketch. Include it in your advertisement.

You may not care for a job outside your present locality, but do not say so. Let the negatives, if there are any, stay hidden until the replies come in. Be affirmative throughout, and it is affirmative to say you are interested in a position in Southern California or New England. Do not mention your salary unless you have an overpowering reason to think it will enhance your prospects.

Watch the adjectives you use. The word "very" is

overworked. Say "highly successful" instead of "very successful." Above all, do not handicap yourself with a grandiose title like "executive" which conveys precisely nothing.

Get started with a bang by introducing yourself as a "purch:sing agent," or a "research director," or a "controller." Read advertisements—all kinds—and emphasize your best points the way other marketers do theirs. Identify yourself unmistakably with the job. You will never see a Chevrolet dealer make a red-hot sales pitch for V-8's, and let it go at that. He might induce many prospects to settle on that kind of an automobile engine, but how would he know they would not buy Fords?

Pay especial attention to "Executive Position Wanted" ads. Plagiarize the better ones without hesitation, but do not copy any verbatim. This is done at times, but employers who read the first one probably will mistake the copy for a repeat by the original advertiser.

A classified ad will be seen by employers who read the classified section to find out what talent is being offered. It will be missed by those who skip the classifieds, however, and you stand a better chance of reaching them *all* with a display ad elsewhere in the paper.

Display ads cost more than classifieds but they stand out. You can dress up your message with an attractive border, or with bold, pyramided headlines, and still use the same general text.

Any display ad is more noticeable than a classified —and you want yours to be noticed. Some pages also are more readable than others, either because they have more news matter or carry the more important stories of the day. An advertisement in such a page will be widely read, but many newspapers make an additional charge for these prime locations. On the other hand, some publications grant lower rates for ads soliciting employment.

A run-of-the-paper display ad—even a small one—usually will attract more replies than a classified ad, but not always. Some Sunday editions are ponderous affairs, and even a well-prepared ad can easily be overlooked if poorly placed.

The New York Times has a special business section each Sunday, and it is a prime favorite with personnel advertisers. Read it for the executive help-wanted ads—there are scores of them, many quite sizable—and note, too, that there always are numerous display ads describing executives looking for jobs. The latter are not labeled "Position Wanted," but they are grouped together, and their purpose is unmistakable. This is a convenience to employers, and your ad there will be seen, and read, by some of the outstanding businessmen in America.

It is no disparagement of the classified section to say that display ads usually are worth the extra money they cost. Still, many a classified produces remarkable results for a comparatively trifling cash outlay. Weigh all of the factors involved, and place the best ad you can afford where you think it will do you the most good.

One or more employment agencies may advertise for you, at their own expense. Agency ads appear in the *Wall Street Journal* all the time. They will recite your qualifications but call for replies to their address; this is all right because you are commited to pay a commission anyway. Take heart from the fact that any agency willing to advertise for you thinks you have better than average prospects.

Executives still at work but scheduled for early release may get a lift from their present employer. Leading newspapers frequently publish advertisements saying a company is anxious to place a talented executive in a good position. That is the finest kind of advertising, and perhaps your employer will volunteer to

insert one for you. Or such a thought may not have oc-
curred to him. Broach the subject diplomatically unless
your relations are so strained that he will be annoyed at
the suggestion. Use your own judgment about whether
to volunteer payment out of your own pocket. The employer will probably insist on paying himself if he is
willing to have the ad run at all. At any rate, have a
draft of a good ad in your pocket when you approach
him and be open-minded about any changes he suggests.

Sample Situation-wanted Ads

Here are some typical "Executive Position Wanted"
advertisements appearing in the classified section of a
daily newspaper:

> Marketing Director, now employed, seeks posi-
> tion in engineering products field. Metals, plas-
> tics, etc. Top management experience. Line and
> product sales, distribution, planning, advertis-
> ing, publicity and merchandising. Acquisition
> and merger. Phone: MO 5-6184, or Box 1234,
> *The Clarion.*

This is longer than usual for a classified ad and would
be moderately expensive in a large daily newspaper. It
illustrates how much can be covered in relatively small
space, however, and it combines the job hunter's personal telephone with a box number, thereby making it
easy for employers to reach him without his disclosing
his name and address.

A shorter classified which would cost considerably
less but is noticeable because of its headline reads as
follows:

> ### ADMINISTRATIVE EXECUTIVE
> Dynamic administrative executive, experienced
> all phases of corporate management. B.S. and
> M.S. degree. Seeks permanent position Mid-
> west area. Box 4567, *The Clarion.*

Unfortunately, this ad fails to pinpoint a job and is too vague to stimulate the replies its arrangement should produce. A more effective ad, costing even less, is this:

> CONTROLLER, TREASURER
> Experienced electronics industry. Cost, systems, contracts, expense reductions. Earnings $20,000. Box 6789, *The Clarion*.

Here is another good one, costing but little more:

> ABILITY FOR SALE
> Available: Smart, dynamic manufacturing and management "pro." Can build your profits as vice president, general manager, or your replacement. Age: 45. Price: $30,000. Box 9876, *The Clarion*.

Running a classified with a headline increases the cost, and employment agencies usually save money by sticking to the straight text when they advertise for an applicant. They also usually include the salary desired. Here is one:

> EXECUTIVE ACCOUNTANT. Ph.D. Manualized EDP system, coordinated sales/production divisions. $15,000. Blank Personnel Agency, 123 Main Street.

Employment agencies will not put a *display* ad in the newspapers for you, but you can do it yourself. Here is an example of a good display ad, one column wide and two inches deep. The short text permits the use of large type and plenty of white space, making it an attention-getter:

> TREASURER-
> CONTROLLER
> - Member Executive
>   Policy Team
> - Responsible all
>   Treasurer, Controller

Functions
* Over 20 Years
  Diversified Multi-
  plant Experience
* Outstanding
  Scholastic Record
  —M.A.
Box 1234, *The Morning
Clarion*

A solid black border helps this ad command reader-
ship ahead of many larger notices on the same page.

Another display ad taking up the same space says
more but is harder to read because there is no white
space and no border:

ENGINEERING EXECUTIVE
Proven ability, Age 43, seeks executive position:
* Economic Feasibility, Engineering
  Construction.
* Mergers, Acquisitions, Corporate Planning.
* Sales, Development, Licensing.
* Assistant to President.
Presently executive vice president diversified
company. Graduate degrees engineering. Inter-
national experience, languages, heavy back-
ground sales, legal, and financial. Box 4321,
The Morning Clarion

This man apparently has a lot to sell, and an employer
looking for someone that versatile would have been
more apt to notice an ad twice as large. The extra cost
probably would have been justified. The ad also would
have been strengthened by listing the degrees and
identifying the languages.

Notice how the following advertiser got across his
story better:

SOUTH AMERICAN
EUROPEAN
REPRESENTATIVE
Seventeen years foreign sales all types heavy

equipment representing major U.S. and British manufacturers. Background of sales in eight figures.
Fluent English, Spanish, Portuguese, French, German.
Thoroughly familiar business practices Latin America and Europe. Age 42.
Box 2002, *The Morning Clarion*

A display ad twice as large—two columns wide by two inches deep—gave this job hunter a splendid exposition of his talents:

MANUFACTURING AND ENGINEERING EXECUTIVE
Top management ability in manufacturing, engineering multiplant coordination, planning and consulting for large corporations.
Fields include food processing, grocery, basic steel, metal working, and recreation.
Experienced in plant location, acquisitions, mergers, and capital expenditure control, including design, construction, and installation.
Graduate and professional engineer—base mid-$20's.
Box 1010, *The Morning Clarion.*

If your employer agrees to publish an advertisement for you it probably will be a good-sized display ad, probably two inches wide and two or three inches deep. It should contain the *basic* points you stress in your résumé—the thumbnail sketch should come close to covering them—*plus* a few words emphasizing that the company values your services but due to unusual circumstances is forced to let you go and thinks you will be a bargain for another concern. As stated before, this is by far the most effective type of advertising you could use, and you owe it to yourself to *sell* yourself in the ad by sticking to facts, reciting your capabilities without saying too much, and using *plenty* of white space.

Of course if you are trying to get away from your

company instead of being let out, you cannot expect the firm to contribute to your campaign. And that brings up another important thing to remember: Do not keep your campaign for a new job a secret from the man you are working for. Answering a help-wanted ad now and then is taken for granted, because everyone is expected to have self-betterment constantly in mind. An all-out drive for a new position is quite different. Your employer is entitled to know that he does not have a place in your future plans, so let the boss in on them whenever the cause stems from you instead of from him.

Finding yourself in a dead-end job or blocked from advancement by a youthful superior are valid reasons for looking elsewhere, and your employer will understand them. What he will not understand is your failure to take him into your confidence, and that is not the way to line up a good recommendation. Remember, your most important single reference is your present employer. Few companies will waste a second thought on an executive whose current boss has soured on him.

The above is academic if you are on notice that your services are due to be terminated, but it is vitally important if your departure would come as a surprise to your company. Therefore, be certain that you extend the same courtesies you expect to receive. Such thoughtfulness can mean a lot to your future.

Tell Your Friends

Spreading word of your job hunt among your friends falls in a different category. There is no courtesy involved there—just plain common sense. You have no obligation to tell them about your plans or your job status, but you may be shortchanging yourself if you do not. Do not take a chance on missing a hot tip.

A friend could hear of a job opportunity that is about to open up. The employer may be deliberating about how to fill the prospective vacancy before advertising for a replacement or calling in an executive recruiter. It will help you to get the jump on the competition by applying before news of the opening is broadcast. Advance notice of such an opportunity could shorten your job hunt.

Regard each friend as a potential job contact and do not forget that contacts are the lifeblood of your campaign. You are not trespassing on friendship when you let it be known that you are in the market. Your friends will get the hint and will let you know, in turn, if they hear of anything.

Just why you are job-hunting need not be explained—and your real friends will not ask. However, there is no harm in dropping a face-saving remark, such as reference to an "upcoming merger" or a similar phrase, if it will make you feel easier in your own mind.

No one should be told you are unhappy in your present post. Even your closest friends must never know—or at least they should never hear from you— that you are in any way disgruntled where you are. Do not hide your desire to improve your position. Do keep the fact that you are sore about anything involving your present work the most closely guarded secret of your life.

When your current job leaves off before a new one starts, your status will soon become common knowledge among your acquaintances and you might as well quietly mention your availability. Do not do it by saying, "I need a job, and the sooner the better," or "Be sure to let me know if you hear of anyone who can use a good engineer." Be satisfied with a brief remark to the effect that you are looking for a new connection, and let friendship take its normal course.

Point-blank requests for help should be limited to friends you know are in a position to give you a genuine lift over the fence, either in their own company or with other firms. These are the men you approach right away, as mentioned earlier. They are your best contacts of all—so harness the power they can wield. Others, no matter how friendly they are, can seldom do more than tip you off to a chance to go to bat for yourself. However, do not rob yourself of that chance by self-harming reticence.

Perhaps you have fancied yourself as the possessor of such a wide circle of important friends that you could step into a new job any time you needed one. That is seldom the case, so do not be surprised if no jobs are offered when you make your availability known. None of your friends may show anything more than a willingness to keep you in mind. This may be solely because they do not know of a vacancy. Be satisfied with their promise to remember you.

Another common error is to discourage yourself with the reflection that you do not have any friends; so there is no one who cares if you are on a job hunt. That is stuff and nonsense. Of course you have friends. If you do not, you belong in a side show because you are not an executive—you are a freak. Your circle of friends may be limited, but it is one of many job sources, and you cannot afford to overlook *any* contacts when your business future is involved.

As a rule, you should not give your résumé to a friend to give to someone else—save, again, for really influential friends who are in a position to do something tangible for you. Look to other friends only for a hint now and then about where you might profitably apply; then apply in person, if you can. Send your résumé if you cannot.

That gets us back again to the text of your résumé. Undoubtedly you have written a good one, but even a masterpiece cannot cover the whole field. It may suffice for a majority of the jobs you train your sights on, but occasionally you will learn of an opening which your sales pitch does not quite match to your satisfaction. Meet the situation with a special résumé slanted toward the specific job.

Here is a splendid example of how you can do vastly better for yourself than anyone else will. A professional job searcher, for instance, will send your standard résumé to every prospect he uncovers. You alone will write your specifications to fit a particular position. And *do* write a special résumé *every* time you doubt that your regular product will reflect your capabilities to the best advantage.

Keep copies of all special résumés you write. Some of them may later be adapted to another prospect— and do a better selling job than your original. Now that you have become adept at résumé-writing through actual experience, make the most of your newly developed talent. Some job counselors advise you to write a special résumé *every* time you answer a help-wanted advertisement.

A special résumé, tailored to fit a specific job, usually is a better product all around. It carries a more personal touch, and it does not tell the employer that he is only one of many prospects you are contacting.

Some executives make a practice of preparing an individually typed résumé for every prospective job that looks as if it might have above-average attractions. That is not a bad practice to follow, even if you do nothing more than copy your regular résumé off with not a single word changed. The information is the same but the obvious typing may convey the impression that the job you are applying for is the only one you have in mind. Of course, if you can slant the text to that particular position at the same time, by all means do. Your résumés will get better as you write more of them.

At this stage you may be pardoned for asking, possibly with some exasperation, how many résumés does a job-hunting executive need, anyway? Unfortunately, you may wind up needing a lot. If you have canvassed the field properly, you will dispose of numerous résumés immediately by filing them with employment agencies, executive recruiting firms, and the companies on your personally compiled list.

Your original version—call it the standard model—should reach all of these prospects as fast as you can get it there. You also must keep a supply of extra copies on hand all the time, because your list is growing and when a new name is added you should take a résumé, or send one, immediately. No one ever expedited his job hunt by postponing action.

The Mechanics of Résumé Production

Special editions will be needed to fit special jobs, as noted above, and adding all the factors up you find yourself requiring a tidy stack of résumés before you get where you are heading which, of course, is on a payroll. So the next question is, where or how do you get them?

An executive search firm (if you retain one), will do the whole thing for you from A to Z. It will write or help you write your résumé, handle the duplication, type the accompanying letters, and even sign them. You, however, will have to supply everything, and that does mean *everything,* that goes to the employment agency, the executive recruiter, and the individual company you are trying to join.

Before anything in the way of duplication or reproduction can be attempted, someone has to type the first copy, whether it is a résumé or a covering letter. Scarcely one out of a hundred executives can type well enough to turn out presentable résumés and business letters, and if you are among these fortunate few you have a new hobby to pursue on evenings and week ends. Pass up bridge, poker, bowling, theater going, and television-watching, and concentrate instead on turning out letters, addressing envelopes, and producing a special résumé when you can use one to advantage.

Without such personal talent, you will need outside help unless there is an expert typist in the family. The draft résumés and draft letters you take to a duplicating firm or a public stenographer can be amateurish affairs, but the finished product—the one you finally send out—must be a professional-looking job. Sometimes a neighbor's daughter with stenographic ability will welcome the chance to get some valuable practice while making a little extra money on the side.

Your employer may invite you to turn such chores over to your office secretary. You should not do that without his consent—or with it either, for that matter. So long as you are on his payroll you owe it to him, and to your own self-respect, to confine your office work to company business.

Of course your duties may already have been reduced to the routine level while you mark time for the farewell luncheon that will signal your departure from the firm. Then you may quietly carry on your job hunt during office hours, and you need not develop a guilt complex provided you do the work yourself, using your own stationery supplies and paying for your personal telephone calls. But do not bring any subordinates into the act. They have company work to do. Besides, why make your personal affairs public property by taking underlings into your confidence? Your bosses know your plans; that is enough, so far as that particular organization is concerned.

Getting back to the mechanics of your job search, the probability is that you will have to patronize firms that make a business of typing and of duplicating typed material. Such firms are to be found everywhere —in small towns as well as in large cities—so the problem boils down to the simple task of selecting a company with a good reputation. A few well-placed inquiries will turn up a list of names, and you can make a final choice by comparing the samples each firm shows you.

A good public stenographer will do all your typing and many also handle the duplicating side of the work. An added advantage is that you can dictate the material, though the résumé itself should already be written out—if only in longhand. Companies in the résumé-writing business also handle the duplicating, and many also type letters and address envelopes. Not all résumé firms have dictation facilities, however.

Any good duplicating concern will do if you have your draft résumé typed out to your satisfaction. The firm will retype it without cost because this is necessary for duplication anyway. Splendid-looking copies on bond paper with impressive type can be purchased for as little as $4 or $5 a page per 100 sheets—say $10 for 100 copies of a two-page résumé. These may be varityped or run off on IBM electric typewriters with special "executive" type-faces.

The copies you take away—and you can almost always count on twenty-four-hour service—probably will look considerably better than the one you brought in. You may have to do any necessary stapling yourself, and two-page résumés should always be stapled. That is no problem, however, because staplers cost little and the work takes hardly any time.

A handwritten draft résumé should be taken to a

résumé firm because the copy must be typewritten in proper form with appropriate spacing, and the specialist knows more about that than the average public stenographer. He may charge you for any extra typing involved, but it is worth the money.

There are many pros and cons about *dating* a processed résumé. Some experts believe *everything* you send out, in résumé form or any other, should bear a date. Others say that the date is unimportant. Perhaps the best rule is to date processed résumés *currently* if you can distribute them within a week; omit the date if you plan to dole them out slowly.

How many copies to order depends on your individual program. One hundred is a good starter if for no other reason than the fact that it usually is the minimum quantity on which prices are based. An additional hundred will be cheaper if they are run off at the same time, but you may not need that many. You can order two or three hundred at the outset and save even more, but the extras will not be of much use unless you plan a sweeping direct mail campaign that will blanket the territory. Even if you do, it is better to start with one hundred and study the results. If they are disappointing, you may find it profitable to revise the résumé before the next mailing.

You will have to decide whether or not to date your résumé and how many copies you want no matter where you take your draft copy, so have your mind made up before you place the order. Also make it plain to the company that you will hold it responsible for the proofreading. Then proofread their first copy yourself, as a double check. Be certain, however, that there are no errors—either typographical or grammatical—in the draft copy you supply. Do that by reading your draft over at least twice with someone else. Read it aloud, slowly and clearly, to someone holding an identical copy, preferably a carbon. Then have him read it back to you.

Necessary corrections may be written in, if they are short. Lengthy corrections and additions may necessitate writing out a completely new copy. Proofread that with equal thoroughness before you turn it over to the professional for duplication or reproduction.

The final copy you submit for reproduction may not be very impressive looking. It will be downright unsightly if even one correction appears, but think nothing of that. The copies you get from a stenographer or a varityper or an IBM specialist will look fine, with every word in place and all punctuation correct.

A photoprint is a totally different proposition. It will look *exactly* like the copy you provided; this means you have to supply a sample that is both mechanically and esthetically attractive in order to get duplicates worth mailing to important people. And no one is more important at the moment than the man you are asking to hire you.

Photoprints are instantly recognizable for what they are, but they will look just as neat and professional as the document they are copied from. They are inexpensive, too, but their great advantage is that you can get a dozen run off while you are smoking a cigarette, and sometimes you do want copies in a hurry. They can come in handy when you write a special résumé that may fit several jobs, or when you are aiming at a second-choice job and do not need more than a few copies for that particular purpose.

Many people consider a photoprint of a résumé preferable to a typewritten carbon copy. Their reasoning is that a sensitive employer, knowing the original copy must have gone to someone else, may feel he is being asked to play second fiddle when he gets a carbon. That is stretching things a bit because a photoprint also is prima-facie evidence that he is not getting an exclusive copy by any means. However, it does not flaunt in his face the fact that a better copy may have been sent elsewhere.

Photoprints also are excellent for copying letters of recommendation, citations, award certificates, and similar material, but they must *never* be used for covering letters. *Each* letter you write to an employer *must* be typewritten. You may send out dozens, even hundreds, but each one should be written personally to the individual or the company addressed. Individuals must always be named when you write to an employer; company names are acceptable in the case of executive recruiters, but even there it is better to address an individual by name, if possible.

Whoever is doing your stenographic work for you can handle the letter-writing part easily once you supply the text, the names, the addresses, the individual salutations, and the stationery. Naturally, you will use your personal letterheads.

That covers the mechanical side of the matter. What goes into the letter itself is something else again—and it is all-important. Your letter may not make you, but it can break you if it is so poorly worded that the employer gains an unfavorable impression before he even looks at the résumé it accompanies.

So you still have work to do. You must create letters that will, in turn, create interest in you.

8

EMPLOYMENT LETTERS

Each letter you write to a prospective employer must be adapted to the particular circumstances. You take one approach when you are introducing yourself and quite another when you are replying to an inquiry. Every letter, however, must live up to the proverbial Three-C rule. It must be clear, it must be concise, and it must be complete.

The letter you send to an important friend who may help you get a better job is the easiest to prepare. You merely ask for an appointment, making it plain that such a meeting is important to you, and say that you will telephone in a few days to arrange the date. An invitation to him to lunch with you is appropriate if you are *good* friends, but not otherwise.

The fact that you both served on some committee

or participated in some activity should be mentioned when writing men with whom you are not on intimate terms, because it is a polite reminder that you are a person of consequence. A leader in a field which is of predominant interest to you may need to be reminded of your connection. "A strong interest in, and knowledge of, Latin America and the peculiar problems of doing business in that area," may be given as the reason for your communication. The rest of the letter should be brief and cordial.

Letters to companies you want to work for but where you have no top-level contacts should stick close to the business at hand. There may be many of these, and it is advisable to draft a good text which will be applicable to numerous firms on your list.

A common error is to write too *much,* especially when you enclose other material. An overlong communication clipped to a two-page résumé may be more than the employer has time to read. Then it is likely to wind up in the personnel department, and you will have lost any chance of seeing him personally or of getting him to refer you to an important aide.

Another mistake is to write too *little.* If anxiety to keep your message brief induces you to omit anything important, you may cut down your employment chances as much as if you had thrown half your letters into the wastebasket instead of into the mail box.

Decide what you want to write; then write it. Say no more, ask no less, but do it in the most effective way.

The most widely supported approach is to send your résumé with a short covering letter, but there are times when a *longer* communication may do you more good. This is especially true with out-of-town employers who are unlikely to grant you an interview unless your sales pitch arouses exceptional interest.

Something more than a mere covering letter also may help you get an interview when you are aiming at a position known to be open. The employer will interview those applicants who most appeal to him. They will be the men whose résumés best fit the job *and* whose letters make them stand out from the crowd.

Résumés, for all their importance, do have limitations. They are great for portraying executive careers but seldom can they reflect a man's personality the way a good letter does. Write yours the way you would talk to the man face-to-face—naturally and informatively. When you do that, a mental picture of you emerges from the effect of every sentence.

Tell the employer what you want to do for *him,* and cite two or three brief examples to show that you can do them. Every employer wants to increase sales, cut down expenses, simplify communications, improve his product, tighten inventory control, reduce personnel turnover, and a dozen other things that will make his company function more efficiently. Tell him which of these you can do for him.

What to Leave Out

Many letters are notable for their significant *omissions.* Do not say you are a capable executive; prove you are by your accomplishments. Make no attempt to *wheedle* an interview out of an employer through a phrase like "without obligation on your part," or similar nonsense.

Never explain *why* you are looking for a job. An employed executive may think he will enhance his chances by explaining that he is available only for good and valid reasons, but he is more apt to raise a doubt in the employer's mind where none existed before. The fact that you already have a position will be evident in your résumé, or your letter, or both. That is sufficient.

You may be tempted to "save face" by reciting the

cause of your present unemployment. However understandable the reasons may be—leave them out. Admit you are out of work when you have to; not before.

Hard-luck stories have no place in any employment letter. You want a job, not a handout, and you are not going to persuade an employer to hire you unless he needs your services. Concentrate on what you can do for him; shy away from even hinting at what he can do for you.

What to Write

Much can be said in three or four crisp sentences, and letters that are short stand on excellent chance of being read from beginning to end. Here is a sample of such a letter, addressed to a company president who may not have a job open:

Dear Mr. Jones:

I would like to join the Blank Company.

The attached résumé gives you a close-up of the kind of work I do as a personnel manager.

Even if you have no present opening I would welcome the opportunity to meet and talk with you against a future need.

May I hear from you?

Sincerely yours,

Note that the firm's name appears in the opening sentence. This is better than saying "your company" and is infinitely more effective than "a company such as yours."

Reference to your résumé expresses your confidence in yourself without resort to fanfare, and it identifies you as a personnel manager or whatever your experience covers.

The clincher comes when you politely ask for an interview, referring to it discreetly as a hedge against the future. It is your own future you are interested in, but the wording is open to the interpretation that the company would be the beneficiary.

The final request for a reply is a courteous way of nudging the company official into giving you a prompt answer and, being nonargumentative, it enhances your prospects of getting in to see him.

This is strictly a "soft sell" letter and insures that you will not be taken for a high-pressure salesman demanding an audience. Such a letter sells without seeming to and concentrates on the immediate objective, which is an interview.

A longer letter in a more forceful but not bellicose vein can be written a company president to convey essential information and eliminate the need for a résumé. Here is an example:

Dear Mr. Jones:

I would like to help you market your line.

As marketing director I would draw on a wealth of experience to help you eliminate surplus middlemen, streamline deliveries, intensify sales activities, and expand retail outlets. This I have done for other companies in the consumer goods field:

> More than 1,800 retail drugstores added a shampoo line after I redesigned the package and stepped up promotion to emphasize appeal to youthful customers. The product is now a household word among high school and college girls.

> I halved storage costs for a scouring cleanser by completely overhauling the traffic department. Scientific spacing of deliveries and keying of output to chain store demand cut expenses $150,000 the first year and progressively increased total sales.

> My four-month study of synthetic fiber brush marketing problems developed an entirely new concept which induced two large mail-order houses to take on the company's line for the first time in history. The firm gained an assured market which enabled it to increase

production, lower prices, and pay its first dividend in four and one-half years.

Because you have a good company, I would like to help you make it continue to grow. There are many phases of twentieth-century marketing and each presents a challenge that I welcome as much as I am sure you do. I have spent a lifetime marketing consumer goods and can offer you both experience and enthusiasm.

Supporting these assets are a B.S. degree from Carnegie Institute of Technology, service as a major in the Army Transportation Corps, and extensive public speaking. Several of my pamphlets on packaging have been distributed by a national manufacturing association.

May I discuss your marketing problems with you? I shall telephone your office early next week for an appointment.

Sincerely yours,

Recurrent throughout this letter is emphasis on the applicant's desire to help the president. It stresses the word *you* when referring to his activity, but discusses a company or a product when citing accomplishments. Any implication that the employer heads a run-down concern is carefully avoided. Experience, ability, enthusiasm, and cooperativeness are offered, and the possibility of a brush-off is never taken into account. The writer wants an interview and expects to get it. He will telephone for an appointment.

Many job-hunting executives also have gotten favorable results by sending prospective employers a letter which does not include a résumé but arouses interest in reading one. The theory is that an employer who asks for a résumé will read it; he may even grant an interview without asking for more information. Such a letter must say enough, but not too much. The following went to the president of a small but growing company, and paraphrased the applicant's thumbnail sketch to minimize the personal pronoun in his background record:

Dear Mr. Jones:

Because I have a lively interest in growing companies and have watched the steady progress yours has made in recent years, I would like to be one of your financial executives. As your controller, I would bring to you the following background:

Experienced in solving financial and administrative problems resulting from rapid growth. Directed preparation of budgets, accounting reports, and tax returns. Installed standard cost system. Supervised credit and collection policy. Negotiated bank financing. Administered corporate employee benefit program.

I am a graduate of Cornell University, hold a master's degree from the University of Chicago, and have lectured on economics at the College of the City of New York.

My financial and administrative experience includes successful operation of my own company; I was controller of an electronics concern and, earlier, chief accountant in a local branch of a large public utility.

This cannot tell the entire story, but it gives you an idea of what I have to offer. I have prepared a record of my experience. Will you let me send you the material?

Sincerely yours,

The principal shortcoming of this letter is that it may produce an application blank in which your age, earnings record, and salary objective have to be set forth. This compels you to supply important personal information *before* you have had a chance to sell the company on your ability, either through your résumé or in a personal interview.

You may guard against this, at least partially, by enclosing your résumé with a letter which contains pertinent highlights of your experience. Such letters often get results—if the writer knows when to stop. The following example, written by a research chemist to the vice president in charge of research in a large manufacturing concern, encloses the applicant's résumé but gives him a boost at the same time:

Dear Mr. Jones:

I would like to help you develop new products and improve existing ones—for a minimum cash outlay.

My specialty is originating, evaluating, and directing chemical research programs with a limited budget. I have done this successfully in plastics, rubber, organic chemicals, dielectrics, and process development. Papers I have written on related subjects have appeared in more than a dozen technical publications; and I have eight patents to my credit.

For a leading corporation in the Southwest I directed programs on petrochemicals and polymers, supporting them with marketing and economic studies which greatly shortened the time required to realize a profit.

On the West Coast I supervised two pilot plants which led to successful commercial production. The board of directors cited my ability to run a tight organization without alienating the good will of subordinates. No labor disputes arose in any of these operations.

Much of the success of these activities stemmed from my encouragement of associates. Everyone in my department was treated as a member of an effective team. We had many problems to overcome, but getting people to work wholeheartedly all the time was never one of them.

May I hear from you? You can reach me at MAin 1-2345.

Sincerely yours,

The accompanying résumé tells enough more about the applicant to make it unlikely that he will have to expose other details about himself—age and salary, for instance—until an interview takes place. At that time he gets the opportunity of dispelling any doubts the employer may have about hiring a middle-aged or, possibly, an expensive executive.

Writing to Recruiters

Letters to executive recruiters should *always* be short, because they, more than any other source, will concentrate on your résumé if they pay any attention to you at all. Send two copies of your résumé when you write recruiters.

Some employment experts believe a single sentence saying your résumé is enclosed for the consideration of their clients is sufficient. Others favor asking for an interview unless the firm is out of town, but you will get one anyway if your résumé is good enough *and* if they have been commissioned to locate a good man for a client.

Many executives have heard so much about the importance of being brief that they think any letter to a prospective employer will do so long as it is held down to a paragraph or two. Here is a sample that proves the fallacy of such reasoning:

Dear Mr. Jones:

The enclosed résumé should interest firms looking for a policy-making, policy-implementing executive in the manufacturing field. I have a more-than-ordinary background in the way of management experience and would welcome a personal interview.

Sincerely yours,

This brief note, which has plenty of hyphens but not much else, went to the president of several score manufacturing companies without producing a single interview. It depended on the résumé to make the job sale, but was so poorly written that it is doubtful that many executives bothered to read any further. The world's best résumé would be handicapped with such an introduction.

Other executives make the mistake of assuming that a covering letter is bound to sell if it is totally different. They try to be "cute" and succeed only in wisecracking themselves out of consideration, as did the writer of this failure:

Dear Mr. Jones:

Executives may be born; I couldn't say. But I do know that management experience must be earned. No one else can do it for you, and there is no feasible substitute.

That goes double in the rubber industry where ability to blend initiative with know-how can increase output, boost profits, improve customer relations, and develop employee *esprit de corps*. You can best learn it by doing it—as I have done.

The enclosed résumé outlines an action-packed management career—ten years of it in probably the country's most challenging industry.

I think your organization would find me a useful man to have around. Will you let me know?

Sincerely yours,

They let him know, all right. He wrote to two dozen rubber companies, and all but three or four promptly acknowledged with promises to "keep his application on file." The other firms did not bother to write him at all.

The weakness of such letters and most other duds, long or short, is that they describe neither the applicant nor the job he seeks. If you are going to do anything more than introduce your résumé and identify the job you want, you must be informative. Calling yourself a good manager or an experienced engineer is not informative.

So far we have been discussing letters you will write to individuals or companies about a position that may or may not exist. You are hoping one will materialize, but are not sure. Most of your letters will be written in connection with a job known to be open.

Companies having such jobs should be written to *only* when it is impossible to call in person. You cannot call, of course, when you do not know who the employer is, which is the case when he uses a box number in a help-wanted advertisement. You cannot call on out-of-town employers either, and you should not even think of calling when an advertisement or a letter tells you to use the mail.

Answers to Advertisements

You should write immediately to each advertiser whose job interests you but whom you cannot visit personally. The job source may be unknown, or it may be a corporation, or it may be an employment agency. Answer them all, and get your letter in the mail as fast as you can.

Many a good job is advertised by an employment agency. The employer may not care to get involved in essential preliminary screening; so he turns the detail work over to a professional. When you write such an agency you can expect to hear from them at least once—promptly if not necessarily informatively. They will send you a contract to sign, and they will not do much about your application until it comes back. You will not hear from them again until they have some good news for you, because they have no time to waste telling you someone else got the job.

When an employment agency advertisement says "mail résumé" send them at least two copies with a brief covering letter that identifies the job, the publication in which it was advertised, and the date it appeared. This is important. Agencies do a lot of advertising, and if you are vague in your response your résumé (and your hopes) could end up in limbo.

The ad may say "submit" detailed résumé, etc., and if nothing more is said to indicate personal visits are not welcomed, go right down there with the material in your pocket. Take a covering letter along with you, because you may not get an interview. The ad writer may have overlooked saying the company is not prepared to talk with applicants until later. Hand in your material courteously, and do not argue if you are denied an interview. But do not forget to attach the letter.

Take a typical executive-wanted display ad inserted by a large corporation. In this instance they need a production control manager. Their ad is two columns wide and four inches deep. The space is used to outline the position fully, which is a plain way of saying they will give scant attention to inquiries by men who just *might* be qualified. Then they say this: "Submit detailed résumé re experience and education to Mr. John Blank in complete confidence. Preliminary contact by correspondence only."

This company has a good job open and is particular about whom they will hire. They expect to receive many applications and will interview only the best prospects. This is your tip-off to write a special résumé and introduce it with an attention-getting letter —neither too long nor too short—that pictures you as a warm-blooded executive with a lively interest in that particular type of work. Your résumé will show that you can discharge the duties involved; the letter will help convince the employer you are the type of man he would enjoy having on his staff.

Steel yourself against the temptation to add that you also are qualified for another position, and would like to be considered for such a post if the job they advertised goes to someone else. That is a first-class way of killing your chances for the production control managership without any compensating likelihood of getting another job with the firm.

Bide your time so far as the Blank Company is concerned. They are not going to be rushed into making up their minds about anything so important as a key executive position. They may not be able to make a selection in less than three weeks. Even a month is not uncommon.

Out-of-town Positions

You will run into advertisements all the time where you have to depend on the mail for the simple reason that the company is out of reach. You will also see frequent ads placed by a large corporation in your city which state that the position is in one of their branches or affiliates. For instance, a New York firm may advertise for a man in their Chicago office. Many firms advertise in publications with a wide circulation and, knowing they will attract the attention of executives in many places, they add something like "Midwest location," or "West Coast," or "New England."

Such ads mean the applicant need not live in that locality *now*, but he will have to relocate if he gets the job. You are the only judge of your feeling on that score. Answer those which offer your type of job *only* if you are willing to uproot your family and move somewhere else. Companies expecting executives to relocate usually offer an appropriate salary, and many will pay removal expenses.

When you answer such an advertisement be sure to add a line about your willingness to move, though it may be a foregone conclusion. Do not make any reservations, such as "provided there are adequate salary inducements." If the salary is stated in the ad and is not enough to suit you, turn your attention elsewhere.

Keep silent, too, if no salary is stated. You will learn what it is at the interview, and then is the time to decide whether it meets your requirements. Absence of a salary stipulation may mean the company has a flexible attitude, and possibly you can persuade them to raise their offering. At the very least, you have some elbow room for negotiation.

Pay close heed to the job requirements in each ad, and ponder borderline cases carefully. For instance, an advertisement says "applicants must possess a minimum of fifteen years' broad managerial experience, the majority of which have been in logic and control systems." You deserve to be shot if you put that kind of a sentence in your résumé, but it emphasizes that fifteen years' experience is essential; so you are out of luck if you have only ten.

But suppose you have fifteen years' solid experience, some of it in the field they stipulate and the rest in a somewhat related line. That may not be good enough, but then again maybe it will be. Take a chance. Send them a special résumé, heavily weighted to stress your managerial ability.

Here is another ad which says "a minimum of an MSEE degree and seven years of experience are required." That is far too specific to be taken lightly. Do not apply unless you have both minimum requirements.

A financial concern's ad saying "experience in high-level consumer contact work required" is much less restrictive. Apply immediately if you are accustomed to dealing with top-flight executives on banking, insurance, securities, or mortgage matters. Seriously consider writing the company if you have such experience in a different line of business. Your ability to deal with important people may outweigh lack of experience in the company's particular field.

Some advertisers bluntly tell you not to apply if you cannot offer the background they specify. Even if they do not, you are wasting your time when you reply to an ad which calls for a degree you do not have, or a language you cannot speak, or experience in a field where you have never worked.

An ad which says "applicants must *presently* hold responsibilities of a similar nature" is not for you if you are out of work now, notwithstanding the wealth of experience that may lie behind you. Aim your campaign at something more hopeful.

Bear in mind that a phrase like "college graduate" probably means a *recent* graduate. You are out of the running, just as you are if they say "*some* business experience required." They want a younger man. Save your energy for real opportunities by skipping the ones that have an aroma of youth around their specifications.

Since your résumé already covers your background —and favorably if you have done a real job—your letter need not amplify it too specifically unless the employer demands something more. Frequently, he will.

For instance, certain advertisements call for an "earnings history," and when you run into a request like that you can be sure that canny employer knows he will not find such information in the average executive's résumé. Possibly he also is a bargain hunter.

You must supply that information if you expect to be considered. An earnings history means the starting and concluding salaries you received in each job you have held; so do not leave anything out. Give the employer the facts and await his reaction. You may be too high-priced for the job he has open, or you may never have earned as much as he expects to pay. Either could be sufficient to kill your chances of landing the post, but that is a risk you have to take.

Giving Salary Requirements

A more ticklish problem arises when the advertisement calls on you to "name salary expected" or "give salary requirements." You may not know how much to ask for, although, of course, you are hoping for a substantial figure and you undoubtedly have a minimum below which you will not go.

You are lucky if you have definitely made up your mind that you want $25,000 a year for your position, which, perhaps, is purchasing manager. Of course you will gladly take more if you can get it, but you will not take less. You will welcome stock options and profit-sharing plans, but you can do without them. You are unusual, but also fortunate because you have no problem at all. Your terms are $25,000 on a take-it-or-leave-it basis; but, naturally, you use more polite language. Something like "I am sure I could make a valuable contribution to your company for $25,000 a year" fits that situation.

On the other hand, you may have no such set figure in mind. Perhaps the salary is less important than pleasant work. Stock options may appeal to you so much that you will be glad to lower your salary requirements if given the opportunity of buying into the company on attractive terms. Or you may be less concerned with what you are paid this year than with future prospects.

You could handle a situation like that much better in a personal interview, but, unfortunately, you have to state your wishes in a letter. So get busy lining up your views. Start by writing down each and every thought you have on the subject. Be sure you answer these questions: What are you earning now? If you are not working, what was your last salary? How long did you earn it? What was the highest salary you ever earned (and for how long)? What bonuses have you gotten? How valuable have your stock options been? How much do you really need to earn? To what extent did fringe benefits—hospitalization, medical services, major medical, life insurance, etc.—add to your past earnings? What do you have built up in the way of a pension? Do you expect a pension in your new job? How much do you honestly think the prospective job is worth?

Study and restudy your figures until you reach a concrete estimate of what *you* are worth. Then compare that with what you think the *new job* is worth, taking care not to let one figure influence the other. The two should come pretty close to matching. Pick the lower one if there is not much difference. Drop the idea of applying if there is a *wide* gap. The job is either out of your reach or too far below you to deserve consideration.

Before you make your final decision, however, recheck your figures to make certain the ostensible wide gap is not more fancied than real. You may not have properly weighted the answer to the question, how much do you really need to earn? If you have valued yourself at $25,000 but are willing to take $20,000, there is no real gap unless the job is rated at more than $25,000 or less than $20,000. Of course your evaluation of the job may be way off, but that is one of the hazards of the course. File your application if your knowledge of the profession leads you to believe that the position is on the $20,000 to $25,000 level.

Having decided that the job is in your earnings sphere, you automatically have saddled yourself with these two questions: First, What figure do you name? and, second, How do you tell the employer?

The figure to cite is $20,000, of course. That is what you are willing to accept, and your chances of getting it if the employer had a higher salary in mind are vastly better than the likelihood that he will pay you a larger stipend if he had expected to hire a man for less.

You may be tempted to pick a compromise figure— say $22,500. Do not run the risk. Why jeopardize the $20,000 job you are willing to accept by trying to wangle an extra $2,500 when you have not the slightest idea in the world how successful you might be?

Remember that what you want and what you have a right to expect are not necessarily the same thing. An unemployed $20,000 executive is fooling no one but himself if he asks for $25,000.

Settle on your lower figure and write: "I am prepared to start at $20,000 a year." That conveys the message that you expect to earn more as time goes on by proving that you are worth more.

In the meantime, let such matters as stock options, profit-sharing plans, and fringe benefits await the interview. There is a time and place for everything, and your first letter to an employer should never be exploratory. He is doing the exploring now; your turn will come later.

Another thing; send photocopies of any documentary material you supply. It could be disastrous if irreplaceable originals got misplaced or were lost in the mail. Besides, you can please the employer by telling him the copies need not be returned.

Finally, every letter you send out must be a perfect typing job. Your correspondence reflects your personality, and you cannot afford to sign any letter that is poorly spaced, improperly aligned on your stationery, or marred by obvious erasures.

9

THE UNEMPLOYED JOB HUNTER

Once your campaign is started, you should get up momentum as rapidly as possible and keep driving until you get the position you want.

Some psychological preparation may be necessary, especially if the termination of your previous employment was a blow either to your pride or your pocketbook. On the other hand, if you left on your own accord, a spirited job hunt may be an ideal tonic. A stimulating experience awaits you in either case.

The mature executive who urgently needs employment must watch his conduct with especial care. "Do not be your own worst enemy," warns the National Association of Manufacturers with a pointed reminder that a *defeatist* attitude has robbed more good men of new jobs than any other failing. Keep up your morale and maintain a positive attitude.

Do not let yourself feel embittered, however much you may think you have been shortchanged. Disappointments happen to the best of executives, but the wiser ones learn something from each setback. They do not waste time looking around for a scapegoat. Neither should you.

Keep regular office *hours,* whether you have an office or not. Get up early in the morning. Leave the house on time. Dress, look, and act the part of a successful executive. Learn to be emphatic without being belligerent. Invite suggestions, but do not let anxiety make you servile.

Above all, act natural. In business, as in politics, you must be yourself, and what you are has to click. Be proud of your employment record, including the job you have just left. Never lose confidence in yourself.

Buying half as many new suits but paying twice as much for them is a time-tested prescription for building up self-esteem. So is eating in good restaurants, even if you have to skip lunch the next two days to balance your budget. Retain membership in your most important club, but abandon the practice (if you ever indulged in it) of treating the crowd to drinks, or going to the races, or playing poker for high stakes. Stick to the essentials, and put luxuries temporarily on the shelf.

Your personal finances require immediate attention regardless of their state. You may wonder if you should let it be known that you are financially well off and, consequently, are more interested in an agreeable assignment than in a good salary. Perhaps the best answer is to act that way but not to broadcast the fact.

The problem is totally different when you have

limited means and are anxious to get on a payroll as soon as possible. If a satisfactory job is slow in materializing, you may be tempted to lower your requirements. It is a better policy, however, to set a *reasonable* price on your services and stick to it so long as you can get by without a salary.

Determining your price tag involves studying the market and the prevailing salary levels in your line of work. Your last salary may be a guide, though it is not always a practical minimum. Whether or not you can duplicate it often depends on your age.

Studies show that up to 75 per cent of the executives who leave their jobs when they are fifty-five or older have to take a salary cut in a new position. If you are in that age bracket you must be careful not to overprice yourself.

Aiming too low is even worse. An executive who takes a second-rate job just to have some money coming in while he looks for something better may have a lot of looking to do. A mediocre post can wall you completely away from executive employment. Do not work below the *general* level of your profession. Tighten your belt and strive that much harder to land the type of job you deserve.

You must proceed carefully, setting your sights high enough to justify executive status, yet sufficiently low to put you in the bargain class for head hunters. You can achieve that by studying the companies you approach and by adopting a flexible attitude. You can afford to accept somewhat less when there is a good chance to go up the ladder in a particular concern. It should not be a Grade B job by any means, but it may be on a lower level than you really wanted. The opportunity of growth justifies sidetracking your ultimate objective for the time being.

You must also resign yourself to some of the facts of life. Job-hunting is at its toughest when an executive has passed his fifty-fifth birthday. It is harder to get a good position when you are in your early fifties than in your late forties, and the man over forty-five has a bigger problem than the one who is just over forty. Nevertheless, there are executive jobs for all, and one of the saving graces about maturity is that the best jobs—over $50,000 for instance—more often than not go to the senior applicants.

A job paying $35,000 or $40,000 is hard to get at any age whether you are working or unemployed. If you really have the qualifications, however, such jobs are within your grasp regardless of your age, because they almost always demand maturity and experience.

When you drop somewhat farther down the executive ladder, age enters more determinedly into the picture. A man in his fifties, accustomed to earning from $10,000 to $15,000, probably will have a harder time landing a new job in that bracket than a $25,000 or $30,000 man has in duplicating his salary. On the other hand, there are more $10,000 to $15,000 jobs opening up from time to time, and many of them have to go to mature applicants because there are not enough qualified younger men available. In the long run, it all more or less evens out. Aim for the job you can fill, with the salary it justifies, and be persistent in your search. Your tenacity will pay off in the end.

Small Firms More Promising

As for the companies themselves, your best field (unless you have unique qualifications) is in the small- to medium-sized firms. The corporate giants maintain their own executive manpower reserves, and they plan to have qualified stand-ins ready to fill an important vacancy on short notice. Hence, they are not likely to hire an outsider until they have screened their own personnel, but they will go outside unhesitatingly when necessary. Do not undercut your own chances by withholding an application from a company just because you think it is too big.

Still, companies with strong balance sheets and fewer than five hundred employees usually offer the widest opportunity to the mature executive. A growing company in that category is bound to need additional management personnel with the passage of time and the heightening of competition. Seldom does it have the necessary additional brain power in its own ranks. Consequently, when business picks up or an important new contract is landed, the firm has to go out into the market for an executive or two to shoulder the increased responsibility.

This is a tremendous field. The National Association of Manufacturers says five out of six of its 20,000 member companies have fewer than 500 employees on the payroll.

Many of the sources of company information mentioned earlier give the number of employees in each concern, and you have been cautioned to record that information. Firms with a labor force and office staff aggregating from three hundred to five hundred are among the most promising mature-executive job outlets. Go after them!

Remember that all of these job prospects are readily accessible by mail if not by a personal visit, and you *must* make yourself equally easy to contact. That requires lining up an office somewhere—and being sure that it includes telephone service.

You really should have two telephone numbers—your residence and your office—prominently listed at the top of your résumé. Only one address is necessary, however; preferably of your office. Employment letters look better when they show an obvious business address, but *both* telephone numbers should be noted somewhere in every communication you send out that does not include your résumé.

Of course, you can get by with only a home telephone, provided there is always someone there to answer it when it rings. You cannot afford to hang around home yourself because you must be out tracking down job leads. But even if the telephone is always "covered" you will not make a favorable impression by operating out of your house. An employer is likely to look askance at an applicant who has only a residential address and telephone number.

Therefore, get yourself an office of some kind, and let it be known far and wide that you can be reached there every day during business hours. Perhaps a relative or a close friend can place a small cubby hole at your disposal. That is enough, provided it is close to a telephone, because you will not do any interviewing there. You will not spend much time in it yourself, either, if you are really serious about hunting for a job, but it is some place to go in the morning. Most important of all, it is a place where a prospective employer can reach you by mail or by telephone.

Some businessmen's clubs provide limited telephone and mail facilities. Desk space can be rented fairly cheaply in all large cities, and there are numerous firms in the business of renting out "addresses" for a modest fee. Such concerns will hold your mail or forward it to you promptly, as you prefer, and they also will make a record of incoming telephone calls.

Telephone-answering services, available almost everywhere, are comparatively inexpensive, and you should subscribe to one for your office or your home telephone, or both, if there will be extended periods when no one will be on hand to take a call. In any event, make a habit of checking several times each day to see if there are any messages for you. There may not be, but it is foolish to take chances. The call you are late in answering may be the one you should have acted on immediately.

It pays to be fairly selective about any business address you adopt. An obscure corner in some building in a good part of town is far better for your purpose than a well-appointed office in an unprepossessing location. Most professional "address suppliers" are smart enough to locate wisely.

Reorient Your Campaign

Selectivity also should enter into the orientation of your direct job search—to the extent that your professional experience permits. Advertising is well known to be a young man's game, and this is especially true with advertising agencies. If you are strictly an ad man, you may achieve more success by concentrating on the advertising departments of corporations than by confining your efforts to advertising agencies. Unless, of course, you are an account executive and can bring some attractive business with you.

Marketing operations tend, as a rule, to follow advertising's lead, and many such firms shy away from mature experts in favor of younger men. There are exceptions, naturally, and youthful candidates do not always fill the bill; so do not write the field off entirely. Do your plowing in more fertile ground, however, when you can.

This may involve breaking into a different industry from the one you just left. Marshal your arguments to show how your background and general experience fit you for the new field no less than it enabled you to succeed in your former one. There are many talents applicable to a wide range of businesses, whereas few are so highly specialized as to be of value in just one.

Among the operations most receptive to mature executives are mining, building, general construction, engineering, manufacturing of heavy equipment, banking, financing, insurance underwriting, insurance brokerage, stock and bond brokerage, and real estate.

These are fields in which seasoned judgment and general business knowledge usually are given a distinct edge over youthful exuberance. Many an executive can adapt himself to one or more; you could be making a mistake if you do not try.

Some of these are well worth exploring if for no other reason than to learn about companies that are expanding into new fields, or are growing rapidly in the same old line, or are contemplating a branch or subsidiary elsewhere. Bankers and brokers in particular often have advance information of a nonconfidential nature which may give you a fine lead on a company you have missed or to whom you applied considerably earlier.

Contact such concerns immediately, using your newly discovered information as an opening wedge. Say—or write, if a letter is necessary—that you have heard they are expanding, or are opening a new branch, or have decided to go into business in a new locality (specify it as definitely as you can), and you would like to be associated with the new venture. You may get the jump on other executive job hunters that way, and the employer is bound to be impressed by your initiative.

You will find similar leads from trade publications and business magazines. Read as many as you can, and do not stop with the help-wanted section. Many important magazines offer little or nothing in the way of employment advertising but do carry informative articles about what various companies are doing, or plan to do. *Fortune* is well worth reading for that purpose. So is *Forbes*. The same goes for news magazines and the business sections of large newspapers. A company's executive personnel roster is bound to grow as its business increases. New jobs will be created, and one of them could be yours.

When you aim for a job with an expanding firm be

sure to say whether you are willing to relocate. If you are intent on staying where you are, ask for a local job. Some of the executives may be transferred to the new operation, and that could create vacancies right in your home town.

Be slow about applying for a traveling job if you do not like to move around or if you have never had to do it and, consequently, do not know how well it would sit with you. Some executives thrive on travel as a steady diet, but not everyone enjoys it. Among other things, it may mean being away from home a lot, and you must take your family responsibilities into account.

Foreign Jobs Present Problems

Similar reflection is necessary when the prospective job is overseas. A permanent foreign assignment seldom provides for home leave oftener than once in three years, which means you must take your family with you. If it is a large one you are unlikely to get the job anyway, because most employers are reluctant either to separate families or to provide transportation for more than one or two persons.

Even if the employer is willing, you must consider the character of the schools, the availability of housing, the quality of medical facilities, and general living conditions. Perhaps you speak the native language, but your children do not, and if American or English schools are not within reach you cannot transplant your family. Such schools may be available, but the environment—especially in some of the underdeveloped areas—may not be one you would like your children to absorb.

When a foreign assignment does not attract you, remember this: Expansion overseas is a sign of business growth, and the executive positions abroad may be matched by desirable openings at home. There may be a local vacancy that you could fill; so apply to every company that looks as if it is on the way up.

Important news about a company you have approached before gives you a fine excuse to file another application, with a brand-new résumé carefully slanted to embrace the latest word about the firm's activities. Say nothing about prior efforts unless you know you are still under consideration. In that case, use the new information as a peg on which to justify a discreet reminder that you are still available.

Company plans to expand at home or abroad usually become public knowledge long before the new facilities reach the stage where more executive personnel is needed. You may get a good job lined up and still have a fairly extended wait ahead before it becomes a reality. Continue your job search in the meantime— you may find something better—and if you need a temporary income and cannot get it any other way, apply for unemployment insurance benefits.

You probably are entitled to such benefits if you have been on an American payroll and did not just up and *quit* your last job. Being on the executive earnings level, you can collect a weekly benefit of as much as $50 for as long as twenty-six weeks, unless you get a job in the meantime.

There are some technicalities involved, and it is advisable to get an information booklet from the nearest federal or state unemployment office. In general, however, you must have done some *insured* work (which means work for a company that paid unemployment insurance premiums) for at least twenty of the fifty-two weeks immediately prior to filing your application, and to have built up at least $300 in insured earnings during that period.

You have to apply in person and substantiate your claim to being unemployed. Your last employer will be contacted to ascertain why you are no longer on his payroll. In the meantime you will be told to register with a specified federal or state *employment* office and to take a job if they can find one for you. Such offices are seldom able to place an executive, but you have to furnish proof of registration before you get your first payment.

All this takes one week. Then you are eligible to receive a weekly check by mail, but you have to report to the unemployment office each week at a designated time and place so long as you remain jobless. The office will stipulate the day of the week, the hour of the day, and the particular window at which you must register.

You will be given a booklet in which you must write an *N* or a *Y* for each of the preceding seven days, the letters meaning either "No, you did not work that day," or "Yes, you did." Then you have to sign a separate declaration, under oath, that you did not work any oftener than you said you did.

This has to be done every week, and most unemployment offices, especially in the larger cities, are packed with male and female workers of all ages and nationalities. A wait is almost inevitable, and an executive usually stands out prominently. Some shy away from standing in such a polyglot line, but others take it in stride. It is not to be confused with applying for relief; this is insurance for which premiums have been paid.

10

WHERE TO WATCH YOUR STEP

The road to a new executive job seldom runs smoothly.
It may be strewn with pitfalls and offer innumerable
opportunities to stub your toe. You cannot eliminate
these hazards, but you can overcome them. Adaptability to unforeseen circumstances is the key.

For example, you can follow the basic executive
job-search rule of never applying to the personnel
department unless you want to work there, but you
cannot always avoid a session in that office. The
man to whom you do apply may require it. When
that happens, be careful not to treat the interview
lightly.

The personnel director of any substantial corporation
is an important official. He may not have the responsibility for hiring executives but usually he is able to

cast the vote that will either get you a higher interview or bar you from one.

Allowance must be made for the average personnel man because in his job he can be a hero one day and an outcast the next. Endorsing one failure can make the company heads forget all about the numerous good choices he has made. Be tolerant if he seems overly inquisitive, unduly contentious, or unreasonably hard to convince. Sell yourself to him and you have a better chance of getting to sell yourself to his superiors.

If your letter to a company president arouses his interest, he may tell the personnel director to look you over first. When he says, "Let me know if it would be worth my while to see this man," you are in for a thorough quizzing, but you also may be in line for a job. You will not know what has been said, of course, but a searching interview usually is a tip-off that there are possibilities in the firm.

Make a strenuous effort to convince the man he will be helping both the company and himself if he passes you along to the higher echelon. Talk to him the way you would to the president himself. Act as though you are facing the official who can hire you on the spot if he has a mind to, and include him in every reference you make to what you can do for the company.

Slip the word "you" in unobtrusively. "My experience in *your* line will help me save *you* money" is far more effective than an impersonal declaration that "my experience in the pharmaceutical industry will help me save the Blank Company money." Do not fawn over the man; he will not be impressed by blatant flattery. Just aim each pointed remark to him personally by talking as one executive to another.

Extend this technique to any questions you ask. "Are *you* expanding your overseas operations? Were *you* disappointed at the action Congress took on the tax bill?" Such queries refer to the company, not the personnel director, but they give him a feeling of status that will react in your favor.

Politeness cannot be overdone, with the personnel director or anyone else, but take care that you do not completely tip your hand and leave nothing more to be said. You already have aroused the president's curiosity; use the interview with his personnel representative to make him downright anxious to see you himself.

Be reserved without appearing secretive. Never expose the fact that you are holding something back, but save a high card or two for the more important interview when you will either get the job or be told your application will be kept on file.

Perhaps you are in a position to bring some business with you to your new employer. That is the kind of information the personnel chief wants to hear; so tell him, but go slow in revealing the details. Refer to it in broad terms, placing emphasis on the extensive contacts you have built up over the years.

Avoid claims such as "*certain* of my accounts will follow me to my new connection." Your listener probably will ask which accounts they are, and you will find you have put yourself in a hole it will be difficult to climb out of without arousing his animosity. Evasive answers will make him think you are bragging about something you cannot deliver. Saying you will only give such information to the president is even worse. Use discretion and make yourself look like a good source of new business without going into specifics.

You are in line for the interview you wanted in the first place if you leave the personnel man in a frame of mind to tell the president he believes you may have possibilities. On the other hand, you may never get any further if he reports that he was not favorably impressed. Here, as in *every* interview, it is imperative that you get on the good side of those you meet. Do that by selling yourself; not by inviting them to lunch or offering to buy them a drink.

Similar kid-glove treatment is essential when you run up against an official's secretary who acts as though her one goal in life is to keep anyone below a board chairman from getting an audience with her boss. Conceal your annoyance. Nod understandingly when she says something, however disagreeable its import may be. Of course the president is busy. Obviously his time is limited. Naturally an important business conference takes precedence over a talk with you. Agree with her throughout, but do not give up and say you will call back some other time.

Transform her from an obstacle into an ally by putting the "you" angle to work again. Instead of asking if it is possible that the president could see you tomorrow, say, "I would be grateful if *you* could crowd me in for a brief word tomorrow." Give her a feeling of importance. She can save you lots of time, and she will if you make a friendly approach.

Every Interview Is Important

Another reason for being careful in every *job* interview is that you never know how much a minor executive, or even a clerk, is acting on his own and how much according to instructions. The company president may have been impressed by your correspondence and your résumé but may still want to learn more before talking to you himself.

Having almost any subordinate look you over can tell him many things. It will not take the personnel director to discover that you have a physical defect, for example. An applicant's letter is unlikely to say that he has to use a wheel chair. Neither will it disclose that he is too old—or too young—for the position that is open. He may be crotchety when crossed—the secretary will spot this instantly—or he may dress too flashily. He may be carelessly groomed. Possibily he needs a haircut, or has an unpleasant breath, or stutters.

The busy president would rather have such liabilities discovered in time to spare him an interview. The applicant who looks, talks, acts, and dresses the way an executive should is unlikely to have such attributes extolled for him by office personnel, but the *absence* of any of these essentials will be noted—and reported.

Your behavior *before* and *after* an interview with a subordinate also is important. You may be the type who thinks it is bad enough to have to wait before getting in to see important people, but it is a downright imposition when a lesser figure makes you cool your heels. Yet fretting will get you nowhere. Signs of obvious impatience will be noticed, possibly by a relative of the president.

Complaints should never be voiced, nor should you wear an expression of discontent that speaks louder than words. Wait quietly as long as other engagements permit. Then if you *have* to leave for another appointment, say so politely and arrange for a brief postponement. Try to make it for later the same day.

Do not let any provocation lead you into griping. A loudmouthed messenger boy or a talkative stenographer is certain to hear you and will entertain the rest of the staff with a supposedly hilarious account of the pompous stuffed shirt who thought everything should stop when he wanted something. Word of this is bound to reach the president's ears, and it could induce him to strike you off his list. Take no chances; demonstrate your executive ability, which includes getting along with all kinds of people all the time.

When the interview is finally completed, thank the interviewer cordially. He may be young enough to be your son, but leave on good terms. Before you do leave, however, try to arrange for a second—and higher—interview. Be polite about this; you may undo all the good will you have built up if your attitude says, "Now that this is out of the way, when can I see someone important?"

Enlist the help of the interviewer himself. If possible, get him to make at least a tentative appointment. Otherwise, suggest that he telephone you (or that you call him) the next day. You may have to settle for something like that because he must be allowed time to report to his superiors. Give him to understand that you think he is working *for* your interests, and he probably will. Wind up with a cheerful handshake and get out.

Whoever you contact in any company must be converted into a booster or—at the very minimum—prevented from becoming an opponent. There may be several such contacts before you reach the top. Be prepared for anything and anyone.

Aptitude Tests

Sometimes a job-hunting executive learns to his consternation that he must take an aptitude test. If you are confronted with one, treat it as the most natural thing in the world. You may not have run into such a situation in twenty-five years, but hide your surprise behind a poker face.

Aptitude tests are cleverly concocted as a rule, and they can be annoyingly confusing, but they are part of the employment procedure in a number of companies. The one you will get has been prepared especially for men in your position, and it affords an excellent opportunity to impress the employer.

Tests given applicants for executive posts usually are fairly brief, but not always. Some firms have been known to put an executive through a series of examinations that consume the better part of two days. These are exceptions, but there is another fact to keep in mind. The shorter tests often are more difficult.

Your test probably will be handled by someone who does little else in the company. It is a certainty that the president himself will not be the man. Undoubtedly, the level of employment is below yours. Nevertheless, it is a part of the routine in a company you are trying to join. Prove how big you are by being cordial, courteous, and cooperative to everyone involved. Do what they want you to do, obey all instructions, and do not object to anything they say. Your *reaction* to the test may be as important in company eyes as the answers you give.

A typical aptitude test includes a probe into your ability to make quick comparisons; computation problems (including fractions and decimals); reading studies (in which you may have to match one proverb against another); spelling (with a host of words that are commonly misspelled); vocabulary exercises; arithmetical analysis; and an English test.

This particular seven-part test is limited to forty minutes' working time. Each section is dealt with separately. You have to stop when time is called whether you are finished or not; but there is a pause between individual examinations; so the whole thing takes about one hour.

The point to bear in mind is that aptitude tests are intended to gauge your ability to *think* rather than to determine how much you *know*. Hence it is difficult to cram for them ahead of time—you have no idea what to expect, so you cannot do any last-minute studying—but some experts say it is better not to attempt advance preparation anyway.

Sample tests can be secured at almost any college or university and in many libraries. Placement offices of trade associations and professional societies often have a file, too, and it is a good idea to read a few over so that you can get at least an idea of how they are conducted. Many of them feature so-called "trick" questions, meaning there is a simple answer to something that appears to be very involved.

When your turn comes, if it does, the best advice you can keep in mind is not to rush. You are marked on what you get right—not on how many questions you complete. You will be more apt to discern hidden tricks in a question if you study it carefully and do not write down anything until you have satisfied yourself that you are certain you understand what is being asked. If you cannot figure it out after reasonable study, move on to the next question.

Self-control is probably the most important factor in taking whatever tests the employer requires of you. Nervousness is your worst enemy, but ask yourself, what is there to be nervous about? You do not have the job yet; having nothing to lose you need not worry about losing it.

Poise is your best asset because your manner will be noted though you probably will not realize it. Losing your temper, either during the test or after it, is the worst mistake. You know better than to gripe out loud about having to wade through a mass of "foolish" questions.

Avoid Pitfalls

Serious errors are being committed from time to time by men who ought to know better because they are executives. High on the list is shaving a few years from your age. Talking about being thirty-nine is funny when the speaker is an elderly comedian, but comedy has no place in executive job-hunting. This is serious business, and calling yourself forty-eight instead of fifty-one because you think it sounds better to be in the "forties" can be disastrous to your hopes. The deception is certain to be discovered, most likely through social security or life insurance records. Those three years you tried to conceal could cost you a good job, not because you are in your fifties, but because you did not tell the truth.

Another error that may tempt a man in need of a job is taking credit for achievements that actually belong to someone else. Say you had a *hand* in something (if you did), but do not arrogate the *entire* credit to yourself if routine investigation will disclose that you were not the moving spirit. Such an investigation may be made. Stress your personal achievements always, but if something noteworthy was accomplished by a *team* of which you were a part, be satisfied to point out your capacity for teamwork. The achievement is an excellent example of that praise-worthy trait.

Then there is the matter of military service. Too many executives brush theirs off with mere mention of "two years in the navy," or some such phrase. Perhaps you were assigned important duties, and if so, they should be mentioned. Managing an airport is a good example. So are personnel work, direction of educational programs, purchasing responsibilities, and transportation control. Such experience helped make you a better executive. Put them on the record.

Of course if your chief attainments were a Good Conduct medal or a Purple Heart, you have nothing to apologize for, but you should not advance them as evidence of executive capacity.

Good Timing Imperative

The importance of proper timing also must be kept in mind. An advertising or public relations account executive should move fast when he seeks a new post. Clients who like you may be willing to transfer their business to your new employer, but they will not wait indefinitely for you to make another connection. It will not take long for them to get accustomed to dealing with someone else in your old company, and if you decide to take a vacation before starting your job hunt you may be throwing away one of your strongest selling points.

Perhaps your most important problem of all at this stage of the game is to avoid being opinionated. Mature executives often appear to be narrow-minded without realizing it. What appears obvious to you may not seem thus to others, and you must curb any tendency to show exasperation with those who are slow to grasp your point of view.

Explain matters, if you have to, but do not argue—especially with a prospective employer. You may win the point but lose the job—because you were too determined to prove that you were right.

Converting yourself belatedly into a "yes man" is equally dangerous. When a company president asks your opinion about something, he wants to know what *you* think; not to hear you endorse what he thinks. Saying what you presume an important man wants to hear will have a hollow ring to it if you secretly believe differently, and your insincerity will be detected.

It is not uncommon for a high company official to mention a business problem and then ask if such and such a solution appeals to you. As always, the only safe answer is to tell the truth. Voice your approval if you agree; disapprove if you do not concur—and state logical reasons for your opinion in either case. If you are stumped for the moment, do not be ashamed to admit that you would have to give the subject more thought. Executives are not expected to make snap judgments on important matters.

In short, always be yourself. When you are hired, it will be because of what you are.

11

COOPERATIVE JOB SEARCH

The United States is peppered with organizations devoted to helping people pinpoint their job objectives and to teaching them how to go out and line up such positions. Many make no charge of any kind, either before or after a job is obtained.

High on the list are numerous universities, which give invaluable aid to graduates seeking employment. Not a few conduct regular evening sessions once or twice a week at which individual job problems are thoroughly discussed and job hunters are put on the right track. Most of the schools also have a placement service—entirely gratis.

Leading business colleges have prepared valuable material which is available without cost to alumni and is sold cheaply to others. For instance, if you are not a Harvard man you can still buy a first-class manual on résumé-writing from the Harvard Business School Alumni Placement Office for $1.50.

Advertising clubs in the larger cities sponsor the Job-Finding Forum, which was organized at the Advertising Club of New York, in 1940, by Charles C. Green, Robert L. Stephen, and John H. Rider. The idea later spread throughout the country, and countless job seekers have been helped by such a forum in their own community.

The Job-Finding Forum is a volunteer organization whose purpose is to help men and women of all ages obtain work or improve their present employment status. Anyone looking for a white-collar job can participate simply by registering and attending meetings. No charges, fees, or commissions are involved. Executives are welcome, but so are stenographers, clerical employees, and intermediate personnel.

In New York City the forum meets at 7:30 P.M. on Mondays and Wednesdays at 103 East 35th Street. A special introductory lecture for newcomers is given each week at one of the meetings. At the end of this lecture, newcomers may join the regular forum for the remainder of the session.

The forum is not a placement agency, though it does frequently have job openings. Neither is it a vocational guidance organization, but vocational suggestions are volunteered from time to time. Its primary function is to help people package their experience so that it will be salable to prospective employers. This includes guidance in writing a résumé, drafting letters of application, preparing a portfolio applicable to the individual job objective, and developing effective interview technique.

Forum Principle Utilized

The forum principle is utilized throughout, and the job seeker reads his draft résumé (or letter or whatever he wants to receive constructive criticism about) to the audience, which consists of other job hunters and a panel of experts. The listeners are invited to state their reactions to the material presented, with emphasis on both strong and weak points. After these comments are completed, the panel members, who represent various fields, present their criticisms and suggestions. The job hunter goes home with a pocketful of notes and usually has a much more effective sales pitch to present for similar analysis at the next meeting.

Such a method gives you the benefit of a preview of the effect your material has on strangers, and elicits frequently valuable tips from listeners. You receive friendly, unprejudiced advice from the individual members of the group, and often you will find that what impresses them will also impress an employer.

Forum sponsors stress that you are both judge and jury, free to accept or reject any suggestions you receive. You, of course, prepare your own material. Your fellow members offer only criticisms and suggestions, just as you do when you listen to material presented by someone else.

The introductory lecture alone is worth a forum visit. "What did you do in any job that was *better*?" is a question that is usually asked, after which you are urged to build your résumé or other sales pitch around that achievement.

The forum points out that if your best equals what the employer expects, you have a chance for the job. To avoid disappointing results you are counseled to present yourself in such a way that the employer will *want* to read your résumé, and to prepare the résumé itself so it will arouse further interest when he does.

Here are some of the tips for job seekers voiced in the introduction:

Do *not* write a job description. Write, instead, about your achievements in your job. The employer is more interested in the extent of your success than in the mere fact that you worked for someone in such and such a capacity for a certain period of time.

Promotions are not always achievements nor do they always serve as examples of your ability. Seniority may bring automatic increases. Relatives of the boss are apt to go up the ladder rapidly. Favorites of the top men sometimes get preferential treatment in promotions. The point that will sell the prospective employer is *why* you were promoted.

Keep references out of résumés and letters, says the lecturer. They are "crutches," and should not be presented except on request. Identifying an employer in a letter or a résumé is not to be confused with submitting a reference, but the forum cautions against naming a company in your résumé unless it is well known. It is better to emphasize your achievements in the industry and give the name of the company only when asked.

Mentioning government employment in a résumé is seldom helpful unless you held an exceptionally important position. Put stress on your capable work in such and such a line and let the revelation that it was for the government come later. The employer probably will be in a more receptive frame of mind by that time.

Other warning signals from the forum include these:

Do not refer to your experience in companies that have gone bankrupt if this can be avoided without weakening your résumé. If such mention is unavoidable, omit the firm name and, of course, its financial difficulties, and concentrate on the noteworthy things you accomplished while on the payroll.

Do not prematurely give your age away by citing your thirty years' experience. Limit yourself to your outstanding achievements during your career.

Do not set your initial target so high in a letter, résumé, or interview that you will have trouble backing down to what you are willing to accept.

Never make an *excuse* for where you worked. If you were with a small mail-order house do not try to create the impression that the only reason you were not with Sears, Roebuck was because that giant firm did not have a branch in your city.

Go slow about bragging about the money you did *not* spend in a management capacity. Sometimes it takes judicious spending to get results, and the average employer is more interested in wise buyers than in penny-pinchers.

The average forum meeting lasts two and one-half or three hours and handles from eight to fourteen cases each evening. Members are discouraged from prefacing their material with a "speech" of any kind. The purpose is to hear what each person has prepared—he always reads it aloud himself—and to judge it on its merits without explanation from the author except in answer to any questions that may be asked. That is good practice, because the average employer seldom wants to hear explanations either. Sample interviews are conducted as a corollary to résumé and letter dissection.

The Advertising Club of New York encourages the formation of job-finding forums elsewhere under the sponsorship of any reputable organization—it does not have to be an advertising group—but stresses the importance of good leadership.

You, as an executive job seeker, may find it profitable to read *So You're Looking for a Job,* a booklet available for ten cents from the Advertising Club of New York, 23 Park Avenue, New York, N. Y. 10016. This describes the forum itself and recites some of its suggested procedures which are applicable to almost any job hunt.

Man Marketing Clinics

A somewhat similar organization, which also started in New York City but now operates in other sections of the country as well, is the Man Marketing Clinic of the Sales Executives Club. This movement to teach men and women of all ages how to sell themselves into white-collar jobs was organized some twenty-five years ago by Sidney Edlund, and it has numerous alumni. Its basic principle is that a group of people collectively is smarter than any individual member by himself. No charge is made, and anyone can take part.

The New York clinic meets every Tuesday evening at 7:00 P.M. sharp at 51 Madison Avenue and sits for several hours, except for newcomers, who are given a somewhat briefer indoctrination lecture. Those interested in continuing thereafter are invited to bring in a draft résumé the following week for analysis by fellow members and an expert panel and to keep up this procedure until they have developed effective material.

The first thing to do, advise clinic spokesmen, is to appeal to the self-interest of the employer. "Don't ask for a job; offer a service." Identify the employer's interests with your own and proceed from there. This involves reviewing your own life in the light of present-day business demands, and lifting out of it those portions of your employment record which are most valuable today. Stick to fundamentals because, after all, what the employer really wants to know is how you can help him increase the value of his company's stock.

You are urged to be thoughtful about preparing your résumé lest you wind up with something which is little more than "the back of an employment record." The clinic, incidentally, prefers the term "sales presentation" to "résumé."

The five essential steps to get a job are defined by the clinic as these: (1) determine what you want to do, (2) prepare a sales presentation, (3) get set for specific interviews, (4) prepare to turn your individual liabilities into assets, and (5) really look to the future.

Much stress is placed on interviews, and members are cautioned to make an outline of what they intend to say—and to make certain that they do say it. Let the employer have his say, too, but beware of letting him "talk you out of his office."

The Man Marketing Clinic believes that you should work up a portfolio, no matter what your profession. Samples of things you did well should be included, and everyone has done something well, even if it is no more than the development of an exceptionally effective letter or a stimulating office memorandum.

"Use your portfolio as a visual aid," says the indoctrination speaker at the opening session, pointing out that it always is a good idea to put something into the interviewer's hands. He probably already has your résumé; it probably is what got you the interview in the first place.

The fact that many of the forums, clinics, and other search-counseling organizations have a sales or advertising background in no way limits their value to men in other professions. The people who conduct them are specialists in sales and marketing—two essential features of the executive job hunt. You are marketing your talent and selling yourself every time you approach a prospective employer, regardless of the nature of your profession.

On the other hand, most of the participants are below the executive level and consequently do not speak your professional language, understand your particular employment problem, or seek the same goal. However, since they meet briefly and in the evening, attendance is not difficult to arrange, will not interfere with your other job-hunting efforts, and you probably will be benefited.

Join an Executives' Club

You may find it worthwhile to go a step further and consider association with an exclusively executive organization. A Forty Plus club is ideal.

There are established Forty Plus clubs in New York City, Boston, Philadelphia, Washington, D.C., Norfolk, Fort Lauderdale, Chicago, Denver, Los Angeles, and San Francisco. New clubs are contemplated in half a dozen other American cities, and counterparts have been set up, or are being considered, in Canada, England, and West Germany.

Membership in such a club, as in the case of job-finding forums and man marketing clinics, makes a splendid *addition* to your job-hunting efforts, but it is not taken as an adequate substitute for or alternative to a personally conducted campaign. Forty Plus recognizes this by requiring members to devote only a part of each week to club activities. Men who do not spend the rest of their available time pressing their job search are not living up to club principles. Neither are they doing justice to themselves.

Forty Plus clubs differ from the previously described organizations in a variety of ways. First and foremost is the fact that they are restricted to mature executives; they are ultraselective about whom they admit to membership, and they are operating business organizations.

Such clubs are placement offices as well as job counselors. They not only teach you; they also line up jobs and help you market your talent. They accept only *unemployed* middle-aged executives, and they require that each man work hard for himself and for his fellow members.

"Our only function is to get jobs for unemployed executives," says a New York Forty Plus club official, in an oversimplification of the case.

Forty Plus clubs are not looking for just any kind of job but only for high-level jobs, and not jobs for just any unemployed executive but only for those who are more than forty years old and meet other exacting standards.

Requirements for membership in the New York club, which is typical of those throughout the United States, are simple but inflexible. The applicant must be over forty, enjoy good health, be a citizen of the United States, and reside in the New York metropolitan area. He also must have a good employment record in a management or executive capacity in which he earned at least $8,000 a year. Furthermore, he must not be on anyone's payroll, he must be willing to work in the club two and a half days each week and—ladies please note —he must be a man.

Forty Plus is strictly a masculine outfit. Women executives looking for jobs are referred to organizations such as the Job-Finding Forum and the Man Marketing Clinic and they are further encouraged to emulate Forty Plus by creating a feminine counterpart.

"After all," comments a former New York Forty

Plus president, "there aren't any women in the Y.M.C.A. That's why there is a Y.W.C.A."

Each candidate for membership must prove his capabilities and his qualifications. The club treats his application exactly as an employer will when he applies for a job. His employment record and other references —all of which must be good—are checked to the last detail, and he is put through multiple screenings to determine beyond doubt that he is of Forty Plus club caliber.

A frequent reason for disqualifying an applicant is that he is not out of work. Many have jobs but seek better ones. Others are on notice that they are to be dropped, or are aware that their days are numbered with their present employer. Not until their employment is terminated, however, do they rate consideration for club membership.

Seldom is an application filed by a man who has been fired for incompetence, or neglect of duty, or conflict of interest, or any other discreditable reason. "Our reputation for being hard to please is too well known to make it worth anyone's while to try to slip by our screening," says Forty Plus of New York.

Club procedures and requirements vary but little in various parts of the country. Basically they all follow the same pattern, and those in the New York club, which is the largest, reflect the over-all pattern.

Once the New York applicant has successfully run the gantlet of screening and investigation he is eligible for membership in the cooperative, nonprofit organization upon payment of an entrance contribution of $50 and agreement to contribute an additional $1 each week so long as he is an active member. When he leaves to take a job he is expected, though not required, to make a severance contribution in whatever amount he feels is justified. Many of those leaving also are invited to become associate members. Associates make annual contributions of $15 for six years, after which they become life members and cash contributions cease. Many life members contribute valuable services and advice, however. Forty Plus of New York has over eight hundred such "alumni."

12

THE FORTY PLUS PROGRAM

The basic requirements of Forty Plus of New York membership date back to the launching of the movement by Henry Simler in 1938 when, however, the minimum acceptable salary was $4,000 a year. The salary figure was progressively hiked over the years to keep pace with business trends; and though the official minimum now is set at $8,000, the present-day member almost without exception is a five-figure earner.

The New York program was conceived by Mr. Simler after the American Writing Machine Company, of which he was president, was absorbed by a larger concern. He was retained as a vice president of the parent company, but a number of executives in his old firm were released as time went on, and he deplored this waste of managerial talent.

167

In a move to find work for his less fortunate associates, Mr. Simler took the matter up with the Sales Executives Club of New York (of which he already was a member) and was appointed chairman of a special committee charged with combating the trend against employing middle-aged executives.

The committee did excellent work, and the Sales Executives Club still is in the forefront of the nation-wide movement to help men and women of all ages get better jobs through man marketing clinics; but insofar as executives were concerned it was, understandably, at its best in furthering the cause of sales management. All concerned felt that a separate organization concentrating on the placement of mature executives in *any* field would more closely conform to Mr. Simler's objectives. Consequently, the Forty Plus club of New York was incorporated in January 1939.

Among the original members were thirteen former presidents, fourteen vice presidents, twenty-four sales managers, sixteen office managers, and nine advertising managers. With this impressive array of talent the new club set about lining up jobs for mature executives and enrolling mature executives to fill important jobs.

One of the first snags encountered was the problem of who would operate the organization. In a sense, Forty Plus was like an army full of generals but with no one in the ranks. Who, then, would man the guns?

To seventy-five bosses, accustomed to giving orders, dictating letters, and having their telephones answered for them, this was no simple matter. A salaried general manager appeared to be the first need of the day, but how would they pay him? Then, as now, managers cost money.

Stenographers, too, were urgently needed. But stenographers do not work without pay. Neither do telephone operators, or file clerks, or messenger boys. Prohibitively high dues would be necessary to keep the

club afloat, unless—as someone thoughtfully observed
—"unless we do all that work ourselves."

The mere idea was appalling, not because the men
were inclined to shirk the task—all of them were willing to toil around the clock to get back into regular
harness—but because they were fearful that they could
not get the work done.

The membership at length decided that the club
would have to do its own work, no matter how technical, if for no other reason than that it could not afford
to hire anyone. Even a dignified president could stuff
envelopes, affix stamps, run errands, and answer telephones.

Typing letters, cutting stencils, and making addressograph plates came harder, but somehow it got done
too. Typewriters took a terrific pounding from mature
gentlemen laboriously tapping the keys with one finger,
but the letters were written, the envelopes were addressed, and the promotion material was produced.

Still, there was the management problem, as who
would recognize quicker than an association limited to
managers? After all, the club members were in Forty
Plus for the avowed purpose of getting out of it as rapidly as possible—by finding jobs that would take them
away.

There had to be an anchor of some kind, to keep the
organization from completely drifting apart. A man
learns to do his club job well and then is whisked off by
an employer, leaving an aching void in the ranks. Then
another one leaves, and another, until there is a completely new roster of mature executives, all hard-working, all ambitious, all ready to contribute every bit of
their talent to carry on the club's work, but nevertheless greenhorns at performing office routine.

And, of course, there had to be someone to decide
who was to do what, and to arrange for replacements

when a man suddenly became unavailable because he had left to start earning a salary again.

Obviously, the club needed permanent management. Or at least a manager. Perhaps an executive secretary would fill the bill. That is what most trade associations and similar organizations rely on to see that everything runs smoothly regardless of turnover in general membership. But call him what you will, Forty Plus had to have a permanent executive around to see that the program did not falter as the experienced men left. That was obvious. Or was it?

Mr. Simler and his associates decided, after much backing and filling, that it was not obvious at all. What *was* obvious, though, was the imperative need for an organizational setup that would insure the continuation of Forty Plus as a going concern with no personnel save its own cooperative membership, notwithstanding the constant turnover in that membership.

Strong Organizational Setup

Once the problem was placed in proper perspective, the solution was not too hard to find. It finally evolved into a functioning line of command, which required that each member account to someone in authority—either a committee chairman or an officer. In no case would any member carry out Forty Plus duties without answering for his performance.

The first officers were the obvious ones: president, vice president, secretary, and treasurer. The club's by-laws stipulated that these officers also would be members of the board of directors, but only so long as they held office. Board membership ran with the office, not the officeholder.

In short order the board of directors was expanded, first to include other active members and later to embrace associates—club graduates, as it were—and today Forty Plus of New York has fourteen directors, six of them elected associates, four elected actives, and the four major officers. However, there now are four assistant secretaries and three assistant treasurers—each with more than enough work to keep him busy.

As the club has grown, so has its table of organization. At the top, of course, is the board of directors. Then there are the president, the vice president, the secretary's office, the treasurer's office, an advisory committee of outstanding executives *not* members of the club, and an operating committee embracing the club officers, the committee chairmen, and two members at large.

Standing committees, which constitute the backbone of club operations, are these:

Membership: Interviews and carefully screens experienced executives who formally apply to join the club.

Marketing: An average of forty to fifty member "salesmen" make more than two hundred calls each week on business establishments in a year-round search for job openings.

Placement: Carefully, confidentially screens the membership to find the right man for each job order. Sends out résumés and arranges interviews.

Job counseling: Helps members to evaluate themselves objectively and reveals hidden talents they may not have exploited so as to develop clear, concise résumés.

Indoctrination: Inducts new members, imbues them with the Forty Plus spirit of cooperative unpaid effort, and instructs them in the work of the various committees.

Public relations: Creates all printed advertising, radio and television scripts to attract new members and employers; writes a weekly club news bulletin and publicity releases; and books speakers.

General services: "Keeps house." Responsible for

all office supplies, forms, and printing. Mails
weekly club news bulletin and the club's semimonthly *Executive Manpower Directory*.

Associates: Over eight hundred voluntary contrib-
uting members, now employed or retired, help
club actives by watching for executive job openings in their own companies and elsewhere.

President: Markets the "uncommon" man with especial emphasis on placing members with out-of-
the-ordinary talents and on finding jobs for
members who have been in the club for a considerable period of time.

New men joining Forty Plus are reminded at the
outset that all the officers and committee chairmen are
active members who gained their posts because of their
background, experience, and hard work in the club.
Each recruit is a potential candidate for a position of
greater responsibility in the organization, all the way
up to the top. Outstanding performance in any capacity is certain to be noticed.

Also stressed is the fact that Forty Plus is a business
organization, not a social club. The New York office
operates on a 9:00 A.M. to 5:00 P.M. schedule, with all
committees adequately staffed throughout the day so
that no important activity will be help up at any time.
The last thing anyone wants to see is a delay in the
speedy placement of his fellow members in attractive
jobs.

You cannot join a Forty Plus club if you do not live
nearby, because it is open to residents only. The membership has to do all of the work. If a club is handy it
will pay you to join, and a good time to apply is the day
after your job is terminated.

Many executives do just that. Others may go on a
vacation or take a fling at conducting their own job
hunt first. Some resort to an executive search firm or a
job counselor to augment or supplant their personal ef-

forts. Occasionally, a man shies away because he is not sure just what the club is. The term "Forty Plus" covers a lot of territory.

Stringent Membership Requirements

Joining is no cinch. The first hurdle to get over is the Membership Committee, which immediately smokes out any obvious lacks of qualification, such as an inadequate earnings record, or absence of proven executive capacity, or the fact that the applicant is not yet unemployed. Unimpressive references put the committee on guard immediately.

Particular attention is given each applicant's employment record. Not every man who has been earning a good salary is a genuine executive. He may have enjoyed a manager's income without shouldering the responsibility properly associated with bona fide management duties. On the other hand, some men may have actually managed a small firm or department but had few subordinates and collected only modest remuneration. Forty Plus doors are closed in either case.

Many men never get past the first interview. Some of them may appear to have most of the qualifications but are still drawing a salary. Such men are invited to return when they actually do leave their jobs, and then the screening starts all over again. A self-employed man anxious to close shop and get back into salaried executive work sometimes finds it impossible to contribute the stipulated two and one-half days' work per week, which includes the weekly general meeting each Monday afternoon.

Numerous other shortcomings, in the sense of membership requirements, are sufficient to keep a man out. For instance, evidence of alcoholism brings automatic, though polite, rejection. A slipshod appearance, careless dress, excessive nervousness, or a lackadaisical attitude are among the factors that flash a "go slow" signal in the screener's mind. The rules are tough, and screening is merciless, but that is to be expected. The club has to be as strict as the worthwhile employer is certain to be.

A highly trained interviewer talks with each candidate after he has filled in a detailed questionnaire, and passes those he considers membership material on to another interviewer. The men who get past the second quizzing are next screened in detail by a special membership subcommittee. Borderline cases, with which individual interviewers sometimes are inclined to be tolerant, are given special attention. Very few doubtful ones are allowed to participate in the final club screening that determines whether or not a vote will be taken by the general membership.

This screening is handled by a select committee consisting of officers and committee chairmen, or other senior members, with proven ability to judge men. They have before them the Membership Committee's report and the references that have been submitted, which must include one from the most recent employer. They discuss each man's case thoroughly before granting him an audience.

During his final questioning the applicant has to substantiate his claim to being an executive and must convince his audience that he would make an excellent addition to the Forty Plus roster. Many succeed; others fall short. The successful ones are finally voted upon at the club's next general meeting with the entire membership participating.

One Out of Ten Applicants Accepted

About 10 per cent of those originally contacting the Membership Committee are accepted by Forty Plus of New York, but sometimes the ratio falls as low as 8 per cent. This may sound restrictive, and it is, but it helps the club maintain a first-class reputation in American industry.

Once in the club the new member has a half-time job with everything attached to it that goes with regular employment except a salary. He has to buckle down to work for the club, his fellow members, and himself.

Immediately placed in the club files is his personal data form, which will be used all the time as the club screens its members to meet inquiries from employers. It contains far more detailed information than the job résumé, but for good cause. Frequently, when an employer expresses an interest in an individual member's résumé, the man answering the telephone can arrange an immediate interview because he has before him the complete employment record and can state the prospect's highest previous income, educational background, and willingness to travel or relocate.

A snapshot of the member is affixed to his personal data form for the benefit of the telephone man—to help him tie the name to the face. Each member also has a mailbox and a name plate, which he wears while in the office and hangs on his box when he is away. That makes it easier to locate a man when he is on duty and to take a message when he is known to be out.

Forty Plus of New York has an impressive battery of telephones which are in constant use on club business. It also has two telephone booths, one of which (unlisted) is reserved solely for incoming employment calls. The member receiving a call from an employer thus is able to talk in complete privacy, and the phone is never tied up on extraneous business. The other booth is for use by members wishing to make an outside call or to receive routine messages from home or other quarters.

The importance of *not* making an outside call in the incoming job booth is drummed into the new member's mind throughout his first week of indoctrination. So is the importance of not clipping help-wanted ads from the club's newspapers. "Copy but do not cut out" is stamped on every advertising page of every publication which is a useful source of job openings.

The new man also is urged to consult the club's regular job-order books several times each day. These books list new offers of employment as they come in, giving all pertinent data except the name and address of the company. The jobs are numbered for ease in reference, and any member who thinks he is qualified for one but whose résumé has not been sent out on it— he is notified every time it is—may ask for special screening.

No such secrecy is practiced with special job-order books for agencies. These list job openings reported by employment agencies, executive recruiters, and executive search firms, to whom members are encouraged to apply direct, bearing in mind that a fee may be payable.

Other job-order books include a fat volume listing employment opportunities in the United Nations, jobs with salaries below the club minimum, standing orders (from companies always willing to interview qualified applicants), and jobs paying commissions only. All tell to whom application may be made.

The confidential nature of the regular job-order books in which the identity of the employer is kept secret was designed to protect the employer against a flood of applicants, not all of whom may be qualified. Members who compile the data are sworn to secrecy, and no one may submit his own name without going through job screening.

The procedure sounds complicated, but it is not. Job orders come in from employers who have heard of the club, or are brought in by field-marketing club members. The membership data is promptly screened, and résumés of the several men thought to be best qualified are sent to the company involved. The employer then is able to set up an interview with one or more he thinks might fill the bill, without having to talk with anyone else. When such an interview materializes the lucky member is told where to go and then, for the first time, he learns who the employer really is.

Requests for résumés from employers who have spotted an interesting thumbnail sketch in the club's semimonthly *Executive Manpower Directory* which is sent to six thousand companies are similarly treated. The résumés are mailed promptly, and the member is told that his has gone out, but he is not told where. He gets an interview when the employer asks it, but not before, and the employer sees the man only when he invites him to come in. Everyone's time is saved, and jobs are filled continually—often at the rate of one per day.

You, as an unemployed executive, have all these facilities at your fingertips the moment you become an active member. Some of the companies may duplicate ones on your own list, but it is inconceivable that your list contains all of the companies who are contacted by Forty Plus. The New York club usually has more than seven hundred openings in its files, at salaries ranging up to $50,000. However, you have to sell yourself to the club before you can even try to sell the employer.

Making that sale involves both getting past the entrance screening and putting in a hard half-week's work—every week. Leaves of absence are granted for good cause, but the club frowns on such applications during the first month except, of course, for unusual reasons.

Only one thing takes precedence over club work. That is the job interview. The interview always comes first. Anything, no matter how important, may be dropped like a red hot poker while you rush off to talk with someone who might hire you. That interview may be one set up by the club, or it may be one you arranged yourself. The club's objective is to get jobs for its members, and interviews always precede jobs. No interview is jeopardized by club membership. The new recruit is assured of this during his week-long indoctrination, and it is the last thing he is told when he graduates into a full-fledged activity as a working committee member.

The requisite two and one-half days' work does not preclude spending more time in the club's offices. Many members report each morning and use club facilities when they are "off duty" to promote their personal job search.

They may prepare a special résumé to fit a particular job, or they may answer newspaper advertisements, or they may write letters to potential employers on a list they have compiled themselves. Incidentally, the New York club has a small but useful library, including Dun & Bradstreet's, McKittrick's, Moody's, Poor's, Thomas', and other directories which are excellent source material.

As a member you may, if you wish, have mail addressed to you at the club's offices at Park Row (near City Hall and a short distance from Wall Street), and you enjoy ample telephone facilities, including the extra, important advantage of being certain all the time that incoming calls will be answered promptly and detailed messages taken when you are absent. You also have the benefit of a desk and a typewriter. The office problem is thus solved without the payment of rent or trespass on a friend's good nature.

Just being active in Forty Plus is a great builder of self-confidence. The optimism generated by more than a hundred unemployed but enthusiastic executives is a revelation to those viewing it for the first time. A magazine writer once referred to Forty Plus of New York as "The League of Unfrightened Men" and marveled at the equanimity he saw on every face. Such an attitude is contagious, and the new member speedily absorbs the same air of unbeatable determination.

While he is developing this never-say-die attitude the new arrival also begins to understand why Forty Plus of New York emphasizes that a primary purpose of the club is to give a psychological uplift at a time when many a jobless executive needs it most.

Perhaps you need no such boost in morale, but many others do. Some men are acutely depressed when they lose a good job, and are in danger of running down hill if they have trouble landing another one promptly. The break with familiar routine and associates can be a real shock, and the mood of depression may intensify after prolonged but fruitless canvassing of job sources. In a Forty Plus club, the new member finds himself among friends who have gone through the same experiences.

13

WHAT FORTY PLUS CAN DO

FOR YOU

When you become a Forty Plus member the club will help you organize your job search, show you how to write an effective résumé, and teach you how to present yourself in the most favorable light. You will be told how to talk to employers and how to sell your market value.

First, however, comes primary indoctrination, which takes a full five-day week. It is designed to help you develop an affirmative psychology, evaluate and exploit your personal assets, and channel your activities onto the highway that leads to executive job openings.

New members are cautioned at the outset to watch the state of their health and to try to keep a balanced daily routine. They are reminded of the importance of avoiding excesses of work, strain, physical exertion, and exposure to illness. These are vital points, because the middle-aged executive, to succeed in obtaining a position, must offer visible evidence that he will stick to the job. Employers seldom risk hiring a man who looks as if he might break down easily.

A concurrent admonition warns against lethargy, depression, laziness, and withdrawal into oneself. The importance of always maintaining a suitably executive personal appearance also is stressed: "The alert executive is always well groomed, he is dressed in the current styles of business wear, and he is neat in his appearance from his shoes to his hair."

The over-all objective is to keep the idea of the *certainty* of future employment always uppermost in everyone's mind so that any member can be picked up at any time wherever he is and be found ready to sell himself effectively in an interview.

Some men are apt to forget that there are times when an employer is unable or unwilling to hold up an interview while the applicant goes home for a quick shave and a change of suits. Club indoctrination prevents that mistake, and it also serves to straighten out the executive who probably has hired many people in the past but now for the first time finds himself on the other side of the desk and needs to reorient his attitude and his approach. He must learn how to merchandise himself in the most efficient way.

An important feature of this merchandising is the development of an impressive résumé, and it must be completed to the satisfaction of the Job Counseling Committee by the end of the first week. In the meantime, the new member is taught the operating principles of each of the club's committees. As soon as he finishes the indoctrination and has his résumé in the hands of a reproduction firm—Forty Plus gets reduced rates and fast service for its members—he is assigned to the Marketing Committee.

The function of this committee is to solicit job orders from business establishments throughout the Greater New York area, and a term of apprenticeship is regarded as a beneficial experience, especially for men who have any hesitance about meeting people. Among other things, the marketing work helps the man prepare for his own interviews while he is performing an indispensable service for the club.

Many members are eventually transferred to other committees, where their special talents can be put to more effective use. As a rule, however, no one is transferred unless there is a strong feeling that his particular forte will enable him to make a more valuable contribution to the club's work in a new post than if he were to remain in marketing.

Even before he starts to work at all the club has already commenced breaking down any phobia he may have that being out of work in middle age places a stigma upon him. As early as his *initial* screening he was asked point-blank if he had any objection to letting his unemployed status be known and, consequently, would prefer not to be revealed as a member of Forty Plus.

Probably he answered in the negative; otherwise he would not have been admitted to membership. However, some men tend at first to be embarrassed about their status and often do their job-hunting effort considerable harm by undue reticence. To them, the club issues this warning: "Do not let pride or other mistaken motives prevent you from gaining the benefit of job contacts available through friends, acquaintances, former associates, and employers."

Applicants for membership also are asked if they can finance themselves for four to six months without a salary, because it may take that long to line up a good executive job. That does not tell the whole story, however. Men often find work within a week. The

Denver Forty Plus Club tells of a man who got a job the very day he joined. On the other hand, not everyone succeeds in short order. The New York club makes no effort to disguise the fact that it sometimes has a few members who have been around for six months, or more. Most of the time this reflects the scarcity of jobs in a particular field or the higher salaries sought rather than any personal shortcomings.

Expert Job Counseling

You may already have discovered that landing an executive job can be a slow, painstaking process before you ever walk into Forty Plus to see what it is all about. You will be cautioned not to expect too much too soon. The Job Counseling Committee, for instance, tells the new member to note these basic truths:

The job is more important to you than to the employer. You attach more importance to what is said in the interview. You are working on a different time schedule from his. A week may represent a crucial delay to you whereas it is only five days of constant work at many things to the employer. So relax. Regard the interview as a pleasant conversation with possibly gratifying results. Treat it as a practice session in which you can develop your ideas.

With this in mind, the committee suggests that the new member consider his club stint as a period of experimentation and laboratory work. This can be utilized to perfect job-search techniques to the point where he will land a far better job than would have been possible if the first one that became available had been accepted.

"Above all, don't sell yourself cheap or into an alien field," says the committee manual.

The importance of exploring every avenue of approach to getting the job you want also is stressed. "One basic rule applies to all," the committee declares. "Be persistent, be patient, and be perceptive. Persistence will carry you from day to day. Patience will bring you to the right job. Perception will bring you to all the places where the right job may lie waiting."

These are among the few *personal* matters that enter into club activity. For the most part it is a *cooperative* endeavor in which every individual labors to promote the club membership's collective interests. No one sells himself while on club business; he sells Forty Plus. His personal sales pitch comes only when he has an interview, but in the meantime the club is selling him all the time.

Forty Plus of New York uses practically every promotion medium in its unceasing sales campaign. Display advertisements appear regularly in *The New York Times* and the *Wall Street Journal* and periodically in other newspapers, business magazines, and trade publications. Thirty- and sixty-second spot announcements are broadcast almost every day over more than two dozen radio stations. Feature articles are continually fed to important publications, and material is supplied all the time to staff and free-lance writers. Individual members speak before innumerable service clubs and professional groups.

The cornerstone of the club's promotion activity, however, is the *Executive Manpower Directory,* familiarly referred to as the MPD, which contains the thumbnail sketches of all active members and is mailed monthly to more than six thousand business firms, trade associations, employment agencies, and executive recruiters. The MPD is revised twice each month to keep abreast of membership turnover, and it is carefully edited to classify the members by industries and professions.

Thumbnail sketches are published under six general headings (with numerous subcaptions) as follows: Accounting and Finance, Advertising and Public Relations, Engineering and Manufacturing, General Management, International Trade, and Sales and Marketing.

Each member's club number appears immediately below his condensed biography (names are never given), and there is an accompanying code number which indicates his salary range. Salary brackets start with $8,000-$10,000 and go up by stages to "over $22,500."

A postage-paid business reply card accompanies each MPD that is sent out. Employers are urged to review listed job titles and individual descriptions against their executive needs and to order résumés by code numbers on the reply card. Nearby firms often save time by telephoning the club. All résumés are submitted in confidence, and interviews are arranged at the employer's convenience.

This procedure helps explain why so much emphasis is placed on a well-written thumbnail sketch. It is the first thing the employer sees, and it must arouse his interest before he is willing to read the entire résumé. But—if he does take the time to send in for a résumé, he is definitely interested in the man. Furthermore, he knows what salary is expected and he knows that the applicant is forty or over.

The member himself decides under which category his thumbnail sketch is to be listed, but this, of course, is contingent on so preparing his résumé that it properly belongs where he wants it to be published.

Each member has the responsibility of supplying the Placement Committee with twenty-six copies of his résumé—six of them specially marked for committee use only. This data includes his club number, his salary classification, the *minimum* salary he will accept, his birth date, and his first, second, and third job choices. The remaining copies are for delivery to interested employers.

The auxiliary information is subject to change at the

individual member's desire—he may wish to amend his salary requirements or revise the order of job preference—and an entirely new résumé may be substituted at intervals.

There is one last bit of information the member may, if he wishes, supply to the Placement Committee. That is the name of any company he does *not* wish to have receive his résumé. This could be his last employer or some other firm which, for reasons of his own that are never questioned, he does not care to solicit.

The MPD cannot do all the club's selling, as each new member is promptly warned. Once his résumé is completed the next step is to plunge into the job search —a new experience for the man who has not been conducting his own and a fresh approach to an old one for those who have been trying unsuccessfully to land a job in other ways. Each member, of course, has to put in half a week on club work, but while he is doing this the club is devoting a full week's activity in his behalf, so his horizon is greatly expanded.

How important this support from fellow members can be is easily gauged by reviewing the caliber of the club's membership. The active roster of Forty Plus of New York—about 120 much of the time—represents an annual payroll approaching $2 million. These men speak the executive's language because they themselves are proven executives. The average salary in jobs most recently held is somewhat more than $16,000.

There is, of course, a difference between speaking the executive's language and drawing the executive's salary. The Forty Plus member does the former, and his goal is to resume the latter. He has done it before, and he intends to do it again.

Yet, for all their talent, most new members face the cold plunge into marketing calls with misgivings. For many, it is a brand-new experience. Even with men accustomed to calling on customers it is a decided change to find themselves asking a company officer if he has an opening for an executive and explaining why he will be helping himself if he will turn the problem of finding the right man over to Forty Plus.

The successful call produces a job order (or several job orders). A job order is the description of a position that is open: the specifications of the post, including the title, the exact nature of the work, the basic requirements (including experience, college degrees, etc.), and the salary offered.

Arguments for Forty Plus

There are potent arguments in favor of entrusting to Forty Plus the task of locating the right executive, and the club's Marketing Committee lists the following as among the more important:

The Forty Plus idea saves the monetary cost of running an advertisement and the time cost of screening the flood of responses.

It saves the money in service costs and fees that are entailed in the use of professional recruitment organizations.

It permits talking only with those men who meet the actual job specifications, as determined by the employer prior to seeing the applicants.

It supplies men who have been reference-checked, and screened as to their capacities, qualifications, personal qualities, and record of accomplishments.

Also stressed is the fact that Forty Plus, being a cooperative, nonprofit organization, does not *have* to sell a man to a job, since there is no fee or commission at stake. The club can afford to, and does, put the employer's need foremost.

Not all job openings are easily filled. The New York club had the devil's own time finding a woodworking specialist for a management consultant firm that had a hurry-up call from overseas. Finally, it supplied one of its senior members, who had forty years' experience in the piano-manufacturing business behind him. His knowledge of wood and woodworking proved to be exactly what was needed, and he turned in a superlative performance as adviser to a factory in Pakistan.

Job orders, once they are secured from any source, are turned over to the Placement Committee, where each is given a number; and copies of the salient information are typed for inclusion in the appropriate job-order books. Then the numbered job orders are turned over to special screeners, who operate with all the résumés of active members. Individual résumés which appear to come closest to matching the particular job are sent, with a covering letter, to the employer. When responses are slow in coming the employer is contacted by telephone if nearby and by mail when an out-of-town firm is involved.

Occasionally, no active member can fill the bill, and Placement then screens associate members, many of whom have registered their résumés as a hedge against the future. Between actives and associates it seldom happens that a qualified man is unavailable. Exceptions occur usually in highly technical posts which require special talent not readily obtainable anywhere. Most of the positions in this category are in the scientific field.

Much of the time, the mailing of résumés is soon followed by the employer's request that one or more of the members be sent for an interview. When a member has reason to believe, after such an interview, that he "has the job in his pocket" he may ask Placement to "freeze" the job for him for a few days. He has to make a strong case for this, but if it appears that his prospects are more than passingly bright the committee will suspend further screening and follow-ups briefly to give him a chance to complete the transaction.

When a member lands a job, either through Forty Plus or as a result of his own efforts, it is an occasion for clubwide rejoicing, and his name is read off at the next general meeting to the accompaniment of a resounding clang from a ship's bell.

Before any job is secured a lot of work has been done. Marketing keeps at least half of its members in the field all the time, but the rest of the work is handled on the premises—with time out, naturally, for visits to the post office, the printer, the advertising agency, the stationer, and other establishments essential to club operations. Forty Plus officers insist that there are no "menial" jobs in the club, but admit that many are lacking somewhat in glamour.

A dignified, scholarly gentleman presiding over a mimeograph machine, oblivious of an ink smudge on his cheek, is a familiar sight. So is a long table where a battery of men who may range in age from the early forties to the late sixties are busily stuffing *Manpower Directories* into envelopes which have been addressed either by addressograph stencils or by the hunt-and-peck system on a typewriter.

Whatever task is involved—and it runs the whole gamut of office routine—presidents, managers, treasurers, and controllers rub elbows with engineers, chemists, and purchasing agents as they get the work done. A water-purification expert answering the telephone may take a call from someone looking for a publisher, a traffic specialist, or a toy manufacturer. Each member is working for the *other* men, but *all* of them are working just as hard for *him*.

Regular club work is augmented by periodic *special* campaigns. Over a period of several months Forty Plus of New York mailed promotion material, including the *Executive Manpower Directory,* to some five thousand out-of-town million-dollar firms with not more than five hundred employees. Weeks were spent on a companion drive to line up carefully selected New York City employers through combined mail-telephone solicitation.

One of the newer activities is an effort to market the "uncommon" man, the man with extraordinary qualifications in some specific field. This is handled in New York by the Presidents Committee, which also concentrates on placing active members who have been in the club for the longest time.

The committee name was derived from the nature of the solicitation, which involves personal letters from the president of Forty Plus to the presidents of companies selected by the club member in collaboration with the committee. The letters request a personal meeting between the respective presidents, or their nominees, in behalf of the job-seeking club member when the firm is located within thirty miles of New York City. Concerns farther removed are asked to agree to a meeting between a high company officer and the club member himself. All letters are mailed at club expense with commemorative postage stamps—postage meters are used for ordinary correspondence—and they are meticulously followed up by mail or telephone, or both. The campaign scored a notable success from the beginning.

Interview Counseling Helpful

Another club activity which many active members find helpful, whether they are newcomers or veterans, is known as interview counseling. It involves so-called dry run interviews, which are conducted regularly to give interested members a chance to run the gantlet of a typical, hard-boiled job interview. The interviewers are always men who are authorities on the type of work the individual is seeking, and they are as intensive in their probing as any prospective employer.

The dry runs help a man improve his oral presentation immeasurably, both by beefing up his exposition of his personal talents and by uncovering weaknesses he may not have been aware of before. These include tactical errors in judgment, such as letting negative remarks creep into his presentation, and slouching in his chair, allowing his eyes to wander about the room, garbling his sentences, talking too much about unimportant matters, and similar unimpressive conduct.

These are but a few of the invaluable experiences that are in store for you when you join a Forty Plus club, and applying for membership deserves thorough consideration if there is a club in your vicinity. You will enjoy working with men your own age—membership in Forty Plus of New York covers the field from forty-two to sixty-eight most of the time, though not so long ago it placed a seventy-one-year-old executive in an overseas position. The median age is fifty-two, the highest five-year age bracket is fifty-five to sixty, and the largest ten-year group covers fifty to sixty. You will feel at home, whether you are a great-grandfather or a mere stripling in the early forties.

You will have exacting duties to perform, but you want to work; it helps keep you from getting rusty and, what is more important, from getting bogged down in a morass of self-pity. You will be too busy to have any time to feel sorry for yourself. Furthermore, you cannot help being heartened by the encouraging atmosphere generated by an office full of men who are in the same boat, as one member wrote he had been before he left to take a job. Most club alumni look back on their Forty Plus days as an outstanding experience.

Undoubtedly it will be a *novel* experience, to say the least, to find yourself active in a club whose avowed objective is to get rid of you and the other members as fast as it possibly can. The time-honored official greeting from the president to new recruits is, "We are sorry to see you come in, and we will be mighty happy to see you leave."

You also will learn something about business procedure you probably had not run into before, no matter how broad your management experience. Forty Plus is a unique business organization. As an active member you must strive to assure continuity of effort all the while you are part and parcel of a team dedicated to eliminating continuity *in office*. That takes some doing.

In the meantime, there is always plenty of routine work, but you have worlds of help from your fellow actives plus the continual support of hundreds of associates and a potent Advisory Committee numbering outstanding leaders in American industry.

The slogan "Look First to Forty Plus" has much to recommend it, as more and more business firms are discovering every day. Companies who hire an executive through Forty Plus usually come back for more. A billion-dollar corporation doing business all over the world makes a point of contacting Forty Plus of New York before tapping any other source whenever it needs a new executive. Some of its top-ranking officers are Forty Plus alumni.

You can give yourself a mighty lift by enlisting Forty Plus club facilities in your own executive job hunt. You are bound to cover vastly more ground when you have 120 livewire salesmen scouting for you all the time, and that is what happens when you become the hundred-and-twenty-first member of the club.

But remember this: Joining a Forty Plus club is only *one* phase of your job search. You should map out a powerful, all-embracing campaign and be prepared, if necessary, to lay down a barrage on the whole employment front. If you do not need it, so much the better for you. In any event, you will emerge a finer executive whether your new job comes early or late.

14

ADVENTURES IN EMPLOYMENT

Middle age is not too late to change your executive career. Many men profitably switch callings in their fifties and their sixties. Sometimes, they are in a financial position to satisfy a long-time yen to tackle something new. At other times, the move is made for the purpose of transferring to an activity better adapted to mature executive talent than their established profession. Often, they earn more money and have more fun in their new endeavor.

Many mature executives set themselves up as management consultants, which is a burgeoning field with an annual volume exceeding $600 million, according to estimates of the Society for the Advancement of Management and the National Office Management Association. In 1962, their analysis points out, there were some twenty-five hundred management consultant organizations and six thousand individual consultants operating in the United States and Canada.

The study further revealed that three out of every four large business concerns make frequent use of consultants. The demand is even greater among small companies, nonprofit organizations, and some government agencies.

This is not a new activity, but it has grown tremendously in recent years. Many management consulting firms have been established for a long time, and some of them are among the executive recruiters dealt with earlier. Even those who would prefer not to get involved in job-placement work often find they have to in order to keep a valued client happy. More important from your standpoint, however, is that a successful consultant not infrequently gets a permanent job offer sufficiently attractive to justify closing his doors, or selling out, and going on a regular payroll.

The demand is particularly heavy among business concerns that prefer to hire special talent only when they need it in order to avoid increasing their regular employment roster.

A management consultant may handle several clients out of his own office, or he may be asked to move temporarily into a company to solve some problem that has arisen. Not every unemployed executive is qualified as a consultant, of course. The client is certain to be particular and will have to be convinced that the man he is retaining for a particular task is pre-eminently a specialist in that field. You may have such talent, in which case you owe it to yourself to make it available—either by opening a one-man office or by teaming up with one or two similarly capable friends.

One of the good aspects of management consulting work is that you will be active in an area where maturity is a definite advantage. Experience that can come only with years attracts many a temporary consulting contract with companies which, by a queer reversal of logic, shy away from permanently hiring anyone old enough to possess such a background.

Whether you take up management consulting as a full-time, lifelong profession or as an interim occupation while you continue your search for a permanent executive job, you have a wide-open field—provided you have the necessary qualifications. If a job is what you are after, having your own consulting business will help. It strengthens your sales pitch because you no longer are unemployed; you are self-employed and, consequently, are spared the eyebrow lifting that may come when an employer reading your résumé notes that your employment ceased entirely on some past date.

Going into such a business also solves the office problem. It gives you a business address and a specific place to go to at a definite time every day.

There are numerous other lines in which a mature executive can open his own office with a far better chance of success than a younger man enjoys. Accountants are in demand by small firms who cannot afford a full-time man but want to make sure that their books are kept properly and that their tax returns are correctly prepared. Accounts of that nature are not hard to line up, especially for a man with an established record behind him, and it takes only a few such clients to keep you and an assistant or two busy.

Perhaps you can capitalize on your personal job-hunting experiences. You may prepare résumés, offer a typing and duplicating service, or set up a telephone-answering and mail-address business. There is almost no end of choices available to men with genuine capabilities who want to earn good money and be their own bosses.

Then there are professions in which maturity is an

asset instead of a handicap, but some "apprenticeship" is required before you can open your own office. Real estate is a good example. Time was when you could go into this business simply by paying a small license fee, tacking up a shingle, and listing properties for sale or rent. If your locality still permits this you could do worse than devote your time and a little of your money —it does not take much, as a rule—to such an operation. However, most states now regulate real estate broker-age in stringent fashion. You have to pass a stiff exam-ination before you will be granted a license; and often, you must have substantial experience in the business before you are allowed to take the test anyway. In some states, you must have as much as two years' ac-tive work in the field before you can even apply.

That is all to the good because it protects the legiti-mate realtor no less than the buying public. Besides, you might earn considerable money selling for an es-tablished realty concern. Your chances are fine if you live where there is an active market. A seasoned execu-tive can talk on even terms with businessmen looking for office buildings, or factories, or land for future de-velopment. Individual prospective house buyers, too, usually prefer to deal with someone who already has made his mark in business.

You do not have to be in business for yourself to make money in real estate. You may be completely satisfied to stay with a good company on a *commission* basis, but if you do well you could in time find yourself also drawing down a good salary. Real estate is big busi-ness, and it is growing all the time in all parts of the country. Best of all, it is not "a young man's game."

Life Insurance

Then there is life insurance—and don't groan be-cause you remember the days when the first thing a man did when he lost his job was to go around buttonholing all his friends to buy a policy from him. That era has passed. Life insurance today is a tough profession, one that wastes little time on anyone trying to make a few dollars by asking people to do him a good turn.

Selling life insurance is not just a job any more; it is a career. This is a huge industry, and it does not have an age phobia. Many big agencies prefer men between forty and fifty-five, preferably with a college degree and a business background. They have learned that a family anxious to safeguard its future or an individual bent on creating a worthwhile estate prefer to put their problems in the capable hands of an older man.

Embarking on a life insurance career requires some basic training, even for the "born" salesman. Most of the larger agencies are prepared to supply such training, which does not take long, and they do not rule a man out simply because he is a newcomer to the field. Experience in almost any business line fits in neatly with the basic training needed to develop a life insurance specialist.

The more successful agencies usually offer a salary plus commission, with numerous fringe benefits and a retirement plan. Pensions generally start at sixty-five, but life insurance is one field in which men seldom are compulsorily retired for age.

One of the attractive features of this work is the cumulative effect of commissions. Life insurance is not a one-time purchase as a rule. The average policyholder keeps on paying a premium for many years. The man who sells the policy also keeps on collecting his commission while continually adding new ones from additional business he writes. Of course, the business has to be sold, because people do not just walk into an insurance office and buy a life policy as they would a necktie or a loaf of bread.

Another advantage is that you are brought into daily

contact with numerous people, some of whom may be business leaders you could not meet any other way. And it is the "big money" profession. More people invest in life insurance than anything else.

Stocks and Bonds

A similar situation exists in the securities business. Stocks and bonds are in constant demand, and here, too, mature judgment is a decided asset. People respect the advice of a man who has been around and has a solid business record behind him. More important, brokerage houses value his services even more.

Not just anyone can sell securities. You must be good at presenting facts and figures—but who is better at that than a seasoned executive?—and you have to be licensed before you can even try. Large brokerage firms provide training courses leading to a license, and once the executive becomes a registered representative he has a wide-open field before him. More individual investors and institutions are putting their money into stocks and bonds than ever before.

In securities, as in life insurance, the general practice is to pay a salary plus a commission, although not all firms pay both. Most reputable brokerage houses, however, have liberal retirement programs and provide the usual fringe benefits, including hospitalization and medical facilities.

Another advantage of trading in securities is the frequent opportunity to deal with important investors, the type who may from time to time be looking for a good executive to put on their own payroll. You can always keep an eye open for a new job while you are earning money in this adopted profession.

One thing to remember is this: You will get a more cordial welcome from a broker if you can bring some business with you. Your executive contacts may be potential customers of the firm, and you should sound them out quietly about letting you handle their investments, in much the same way that you utilized them in your job hunt. Here, as in almost every phase of life, it pays to know important people—and to capitalize on that acquaintance.

One of the fastest-growing branches of the investment field is the mutual fund line. Tens of thousands of investors, large and small, are going in for mutual funds these days. Mutual fund selling also requires a license, and the larger companies provide the necessary training that makes passing the examination a relatively simple matter for a man with the kind of judgment possessed by the average mature executive. Look into it. You may earn a lot of money in a profession where your age will help you succeed.

Temporary Management Jobs

For the executive who would prefer to keep away from sales work there are multiple opportunities in the temporary management area. Here you can continue your search for a permanent job while earning some money and keeping "in practice" at the same time.

Part-time hiring has long flourished among firms needing occasional clerical, stenographic, and general office help, but now the field is broadening. Many companies find themselves with cyclical openings for management personnel. They need an executive or two for several weeks each quarter, or for several months during the year, but cannot afford to pay them all the time. You may provide an ideal solution to such problems if you are willing to work when they need you and to drop out when they do not.

A new type of employment agency has sprung up to fill this need by offering its placement facilities to industry and to unemployed executives. They are to be found in most large cities, and many of them offer exceptional services. Here is the way the more successful agencies operate:

You register with them, stating the type of work you want and the part-time salary you are willing to accept. The agency looks around for a suitable post, and as soon as one is lined up you are hired by the agency and then "loaned" to the client for a somewhat higher stipend. The difference represents the agency's fee or commission for its services. *You* pay nothing.

During your working period you are paid weekly, fortnightly, or monthly by the agency for the full amount of your stipulated salary, minus social security deductions, just as though you were a full-time employee. Sometimes, it is possible to step from one assignment directly into another, and you may remain on the agency payroll indefinitely.

Occasionally, a temporary stint produces a permanent job offer, and if you accept, the agency terminates its contract with you and charges the company a "finder's" commission. Only rarely will you be called upon to pay anything yourself.

Electronic data processing supervisors are in especial demand for such temporary positions. Skilled management and professional men also are needed periodically in the realms of finance, accounting, sales analysis, sales management, various types of research, electrical engineering, electronics, marketing, patents, employee and labor relations, systems analysis, and production control. It may pay you to file your résumé with temporary management agencies in your city.

Opportunities Overseas

Overseas service is another, though more limited, field for temporary executive employment. The United Nations is continually searching for talented executives in numerous lines for one- and two-year assignments abroad. The pay usually is good, but the requirements are exacting, and fluency in a foreign language often is a must. Engineers, plant managers, technicians, economists, teachers, and market researchers are most in demand. Complete information may be obtained from the U.N. Secretariat.

Various American government agencies have periodic short-term work overseas for highly skilled executives, and you can learn about them from the nearest U.S. Employment Service office. However, some of the major American aid and development programs abroad rely heavily on private industry to get the ball rolling. Engineering, construction, and management consultant firms with overseas experience are called upon to make detailed surveys of specific areas to determine the feasibility of contemplated projects. This frequently necessitates hiring capable talent, for which the pay is liberal while the job lasts.

You may earn $15,000 to $25,000 or more for ten or twelve months' work. You may also get a new assignment to take up where a concluding one leaves off, but even if you do not, you have another *current* achievement which will look well in your résumé and probably will swing some weight with other prospective employers.

Lining up a job like this takes thorough canvassing and considerable patience. Government contracts in peacetime are awarded only after prolonged study, and there are almost always several big companies bidding for the work. Each concern tries, in the meantime, to get the necessary temporary personnel on the string without actually hiring anyone. You will not get the job unless the company lands the contract; so it pays to get yourself screened by as many as possible. You will have ample time for that because the government is not famous for making up its mind quickly.

You will find two good features about these temporary jobs if you are willing to work abroad: First, they almost always pay well and, second, by the time the contract has run its course you may have lined up a permanent post with another company on the scene. A background in engineering, accounting, marketing, or research is almost always helpful. Knowledge of one or more foreign languages is a definite asset.

Whether it is advisable to take a temporary job out of the country is another matter. The income, the chance to build up a new (albeit short) business record, and the possibility of making a long-term connection overseas are attractions not lightly to be dismissed. However, there also is a debit side. When you leave the country you cannot do any job hunting at home, and should you be unable to line up something new while you are away you will have to start all over again when you return. Furthermore, you will be out of touch with things; and, of course, you will be older.

The time will not be wasted, because you will earn some money and you will gain valuable new experience. Still, another year or so added to an already mature age will not help your permanent job prospects. Perhaps the answer depends on your financial situation. If you could use the money, it might pay you to apply to companies in the business. You can get their names from professional associations, government agencies, your congressman or, often, simply by reading newspapers and trade publications.

Government Positions

Of course, not all government jobs involve overseas assignments. Executive talent is needed here at home as well, and middle age is no barrier if you are able to convince officials with hiring authority that you are the man they want.

There are not many well-paying executive jobs in federal, state, or municipal governments, and the comparatively few positions that carry an executive salary are usually political plums. The men who get them are expected to know something about the work, but they also have to know the right people.

If you are interested in such a job, almost the only feasible approach is to sell yourself to an important official who has a post to fill. Unfortunately, he has far less leeway about hiring than an employer enjoys in private industry. After *you* have sold him, *he* will have to sell his superiors, and he will have to be definitely anxious to obtain your services before he plunges into the battle of getting the right to add you to his staff.

Such a battle is inevitable, because every desirable government job attracts droves of hopeful applicants who bombard the department having the opening with endorsements from their congressman, their senators, and as many political figures as they can line up. Consequently, you will be only one of many seeking the appointment.

Many an official shuns such controversies because he is afraid of making enemies, and the easiest way out for him is to give the job to the applicant who has the strongest backing. A strong-willed officeholder will fight for the man he wants, and you may be the winner. It is worth a try when an attractive post is involved, but you will be vulnerable the next time there is a change in administration. Positions of your type have little civil service protection.

Summing Up

The point to remember is that executive jobs are to be found almost everywhere a *determined* man looks for them. Some are better than others, but all have their good points and their drawbacks. You are certain to run into strong competition for every single one, but you are an executive, and executives thrive on competition. It adds zest to life.

Executive job-hunting is an adventure, and you should make the most of the exhilaration it affords. There are not nearly so many dead ends as you probably surmised when you commenced your search. You may have to explore many channels before you reach your objective, but in later years you will look back on this campaign as possibly the most interesting period of your life.

Few experiences can offer so many possibilities. You can fight unceasingly for the exact type of job you want —refusing to take anything less. Or you can launch into a completely different field where you pit your mettle and your executive talent against a brand-new business challenge.

You can open up your own business—either permanently or to create a stepping stone to the salaried job of your choice. Or you may prefer to work two or three days a week while you press on to a full-time post. You may be attracted to a temporary assignment, at home or abroad, where you will learn much that is new and will be paid a salary while you are learning.

Every job interview you get will add something to your life. Later, in retrospect, you will chuckle at the frustration you felt over interviews you failed to get, jobs that eluded your grasp, and apparent opportunities that turned out to be nothing more than mirages. Most of all, you will enjoy looking back on the interview that *did* produce the job you wanted.

For the moment, however, you are still job hunting, and you must put your heart into your campaign. The world is challenging you to prove your worth; accept that challenge and compel industry to recognize the exceptional qualifications you possess. You have talent to offer, and the demand for talent is inexhaustible.

You have only to knock on the *right* door and it will be opened to you. Intensify your search. Widen the scope of your campaign. Do more for yourself each day than you did the day before. Be undefeatable; the man who cannot be beaten will not be. There *is* an executive job for you. Go out and get it!

INDEX